Michele Dykstra

The Pink
Houseguest

Prologue

The path from normal to completely unimaginable can be rather short. You hold in your hands a very personal invitation to walk with me through a series of events that is at once hard to believe and frightening in its possibility. Because as each of us amble through our lives, we seldom stop to think that one small misstep, one oversight, one mistake or one virus could change our direction so completely as to change everything we know going forward. The pages, words, pictures and emotions we are about to share illustrate a very unexpected journey for all those involved.

Ideally, I'd brew up a pot of French pressed coffee and we'd sit comfortably together at my kitchen table as friends sharing these intimate details. Perhaps after catching up and smiling and topping off our coffee, you'd inquire about my friend Katy. And while I have many stories, none are quite as pink and lovely, shocking or compelling as the story I'm about to share about Katy and how I came to have a pink houseguest.

While the beginning of my story takes mere seconds, the briefest passing of time, as I begin to share with you, it is as though I'm transported through time to a place where she and I would laugh together and enjoy a friendship built on commonalities. Smiling Katy with her essential oils, braided hair and homemade jewelry, at the gym or at the park, with her swollen belly anticipating baby #3.

But that doesn't begin to explain what happened on President's Day.

I am so excited to spend the day with my boys that I'm grinning like a fool. And it's a great day to be inside because it's really chilly outside so we've decided to hang out in our pajamas. In my fifteen years in Texas I think this is the hardest winter I can recall. Like I said, a perfect morning to stay inside. The boys are doing just that all snuggled in front of the TV enjoying this lazy morning in their pajamas. My son Sam is six and beside him is four-year-old Kendrick. Technically, I am Kendrick's nanny, but he feels just like family. In fact, these two boys have known each other for so long they think they're "brudders". And in our little world, we agree. Although two boys are great, three might be even better, so Logan is coming over in a couple hours for added fun. We'll probably build a giant fort in the game room and get out the LEGOs and the NERF guns.

The boys are highly entertained and their giggles follow me upstairs to check my email and see what is going on in the world. A Faceboook post from my friend Al that his wife Katy is in the hospital catches my attention. Katy is not a firm believer in the medical system and has no medical insurance. I'm instantly concerned. Only five days prior, Katy had a homebirth, welcoming a healthy, beautiful baby girl, Arielle, into this world. On the morning she was born, Katy even texted me a picture of her. I was hoping to go over and meet the new and highly anticipated family member soon but was giving them family time to bond. Knowing Katy, she probably got dehydrated and needs fluids and she'll be home for dinner. Decision made, we'll all go visit her later that day, take her some magazines and cheer her up. They could probably use a casserole too. Her whole family is probably hanging out in her room so I'll call and see if they need me to bring anything in particular.

Without hesitation, I pick up the phone and make the call that will start it all. A call to Katy's husband Al offering help is met with a request to go fetch the baby. Of course I agree and so it begins.

A quick call to Karen and she and Logan will come a little later so I can go pick up Katy's baby. Without hesitation, the boys and I throw on some clothes for this new adventure. We all bundle up and Sam and Kendrick load into the back seat so we can make the short drive to Katy's house. Passing the corner Kroger grocery store we turn into her subdivision to the two-story rental house in a cul-de-sac. In the years I have known Katy and Al, I have probably helped them move at least four times. But I missed out on this move just prior to Hurricane Ike. I reminisce at the memories of lugging plastic trash bags of clothes and countless trips to the next destination. Parking in the driveway and armed with Matchbox cars, the boys stay in the car playing as I prepare to meet and fetch Baby Arielle.

Grandpa Ike answers the door cradling a pink bundle asleep in his arms and he has a little smile on his face that leads me to believe he'd be fine just standing there with that baby girl in his arms all day. Arielle has never left the house before and the hand-me-down car seat is somewhere in the cold, dark, cluttered garage. Boxes and toys and high chairs and strollers and clothes and bikes and at last, a car seat. Securing the base behind my driver's seat the boys and I discuss what we will do with the baby coming to visit. Sam is greatly disappointed to learn that she won't be playing with them and can't even crawl.

There are no baby supplies at my house so I grab a plastic grocery sack and toss in four diapers, some wipes, a burp cloth, a couple gowns and a blanket. A tub of formula and a solitary capless baby bottle full of water on the counter are included in a makeshift diaper bag. That should last a few hours. Ike begrudgingly releases his charge so he can join the rest of the family at the hospital. Placing Arielle in the carrier I gingerly strap her tiny form in the five-point harness in awe of her newborn size. It has been many years since I handled such a tiny baby. Buckling myself in, I feel a tremendous sense of responsibility. The Jeep is loaded with all my precious cargo as we navigate down the driveway and embark on Arielle's first car trip and an unforgettable journey.

Katy has Strep. Strep A to be precise. Al just called me at home and told me I need to bring the baby to the hospital immediately to have her tested for Strep. At least when I take the baby to the hospital I can go pop in and see Katy. The hospital has a Minor Emergency location they want me to use. Quick arrangements for the boys and then I load Arielle up again for her second car trip in one day and we head west down Kingwood Drive.

I check her in at the office and wait as Al's folks arrive to sit with me and gaze at baby Arielle. His tiny Italian mother Tina, with her long red hair and full-length fur coat is the first to greet me and take Arielle. Ike stands stoically by her side. I hand the infant to her paternal grandmother and watch as Tina rocks the baby and starts to cry.

"A baby has to have a mother. A baby has to have a mother."

Over and over she chants this line with gentle tears streaking her cheeks. She is shaking and I'm beginning to think she might drop the baby.

"Tina, are you alright?" I inquire.

"No."

"Let me get you some water. Have you eaten anything?"

"I cannot eat. This is terrible, just terrible."

"What's terrible Tina?"

"Katy. They have given her less than a 5% chance of survival."

"WHAT?"

I'm incredulous. Dumbfounded. Shocked. She can't be right. This is all wrong. I'm sure I've misheard her and she's simply confused. Tina hands me the baby as her emotions get the better of her and her whole body begins to shake. She is not confidant in holding her brand new granddaughter. I'm busy processing this new information. Katy? Healthy, active, holistic Katy? Katy who exercises and eats right and worked right up until she delivered Arielle? That Katy? My Katy? My friend, my Mom's group President, my confidante, my massage therapist? Five percent chance of survival didn't sound good.

Turns out 5% was optimistic.

The nurse tells us the baby is too young for them to assess and that I need to go across the parking lot to the ER. But now I'm tired and frustrated and a little numb with shock. The baby starts to fuss. What this young lady needs is a bottle and a nap. Daddy Al agrees and little Miss Arielle and I head home.

But this is not to be our last trip out that day. For the third time, Arielle and I get to go on a car ride. Our second trip to the Kingwood Medical Center where Al has arranged a private room in the ER for Arielle. He has also found a doctor that will come perform the exam quickly. When we arrive the designated room is full of people and some new faces emerge during this crisis. Ike and Tina are there looking exhausted. Lucille, Katy's mother, visiting from Michigan simply looks confused. Her short brown hair is a mess and she stares at the ground. For the first time, I meet Al's beautiful sister Betta and her amazing husband Tom. They have interrupted their vacation and flown in from Colorado to be by Al and Katy's side. Katy adores Betta and Tom and I am so pleased to meet them and feel an instant kinship. Baby Arielle shares a middle name in honor of her petite, dark-haired Aunt Betta. I like them instantly and they are quick to ask what I need and rush me to the store to obtain it while the rest of the family waits for news.

This is also when I meet Alice the midwife. She takes charge of the situation and chides me for not having a properly packed diaper bag versus the sack I show up with. The midwife quickly assesses the baby and determines Arielle's umbilical stump needs attention. I totally understand how someone could forget something as mundane as cleaning her belly button, but there is an odor. Now everyone in the room debates over what we should clean it with and I'm just trying to be helpful and it dawns on me, I can't win. I'm trying to please Katy and Al and do as I think they'd like things to be done but the grandparents are weighing in and Alice makes the decision. Tom and I head out to buy rubbing alcohol, a brand new car seat and assorted supplies for his beautiful new niece.

Then some good news. The doctor returns, lessening the tension in the room with the results that baby Arielle is healthy and does not have Strep A. I decide to leave the doting family with their new baby and pop on up to see Katy. There's a bounce in my step as I find my way through the newly-constructed hospital maze to go see my friend. The Kingwood Medical Center ICU is modern and clean with that brand-new smell. I pass through the ICU waiting room and my heart goes out to the weary and broken inhabitants clustered in chairs, waiting for news. A quick hand wash before I enter the sounds and smells of the ICU hall and head to my right and Room 16. No one else is visiting her dimly lit room, a nurse is busying herself in a corner and I walk in and start talking to Katy.

"Hey Katy, it's Michele. I came to visit."

As I stand by the bed, I look down at my friend and I am appalled. This is not my Katy. Other than her hair, I cannot identify her by any of her features. She is a huge lump and bloated like road kill. Her face is masked largely by the tube in her throat and what I can see is swollen and distended. Her eyes are puffy slits. Her hands have expanded to the point the skin has turned a weird dark pink color and her feet are inflated. Where do I touch her? Her shoulder? Katy believes in the healing power of touch. If there is anything I could do for her, it would be that, the simple gesture of sharing warmth and loving energy. I place my hand on her exposed shoulder and she feels all wrong. She's mushy and her skin isn't elastic or firm. The phrase "less than a 5% chance of survival" starts playing in my head. The Strep A in her bloodstream has ravaged her so thoroughly she has complete organ failure and now is laying in this hospital bed, unidentifiable, hooked up to every imaginable machine, in a coma. What is happening? How could this happen? What do I say? If she can hear me, if in any infinitesimal way she can sense my presence, what can I give her now?

"Katy," I start "Girl you look like hell. And your hair! Seriously, you have got to get better and get up so we can do something about those roots!"

The ICU nurse pauses mid-task and peers at me over her shoulder. I could sense her disbelief over my words and the overhanging tension of "less than a 5% chance of survival".

But that was their reality.

Katy and I were having some girlfriend talk. We share strong beliefs and our friendship is cemented over touch, love and laughter. One of Katy's greatest gifts is that her hands make magic as a massage therapist. She's one of those touchy-feely types with a quick hug or just a squeeze of your arm to say hello. Her innate ability to massage and manipulate worries and aches away was a Godsend during my struggle with infertility, a high risk but successful pregnancy and sub-sequent devastating divorce. Passion is another gift in Katy's life that shows up in all she does. She loves her husband Al. She loves her kids. She loves her job. She loves her life. She loves her dogs and her garden and being active and work-ing out and karaoke and going to the beach and laughing with friends. Her love of life and enthusiasm are qualities that light up a room. She and Al share a sense of humor. As an earth mother, laughter and touch are the warm tools of her trade and you can feel the love in every movement. All these thoughts race through my mind as I try to reconcile the woman before and the woman before me now. I spend a few more minutes talking and touching Katy's shoulder and then make my way back to the ER.

There is no lightness in my step this time and my face reg-isters overwhelming shock and dismay. Collecting the baby and her few things, we leave all of her family in the stuffy, miserable waiting room. Heading home with her baby, her newborn, her culmination of touch, love and laughter de-livered in the form of a 9 pound 13 ounce baby girl named Arielle.

That detail stays firm in my memory, yet the rest unfolds like a dream-soaked blur. I sit in the loveseat with Arielle in my arms and she sleeps. Logan brought his mom Karen to the playdate so I could run around with the baby. Karen and the children are full of questions and concern. I'm stunned. No one understands how bad off Katy is or the severity of her situation. No one mentions coming by to pick up the baby. But then again, they can't. Katy's mom, Lucille, is a wreck. An absolute, discombobulated disaster and afraid to leave the ICU in case Katy wakes up. Al's Mom and Step-dad, Tina and Ike are similarly distraught and trying to support Al as he faces heart-breaking decisions and a minefield of medical jargon and bureaucracy. Al's sister, Betta and her husband are also holing up in the ICU waiting room bolstering Al as they all hope for better news. Now this family, Katy's family, huddles together in a sterile room with awkward chairs and wear the faces of grief and uncertainty. Who is left? Amber? Katy's eldest child Amber is fifteen and certainly capable but also a high school student. Katy's best friend? Katy has really good friends but maybe not a best friend. The other Mom's we know in our Mom's group or in general have multiple children or very small, needy kiddos. I am able. Even more, I am willing. So it seems I will be caring for Arielle for the immediate future.

I don't remember making any phone calls or asking for any help, but all of a sudden, everything I need to hap- pen, starts happening. People start arriving with diapers, bottles, formula, a bouncer, a bassinet, a swing, offers of help, hand-me-downs and a bag of stuff from Katy's house. My neighbor Krystal has been assigned my Go-to Mama for whatever need arises. After Krystal puts her kids down for the night she comes over to help. She brings a lot of laugh- ter to a very overwhelming situation.

Arielle is nestled into her cheetah-print "recliner" and I should go to bed. But I simply can't. Whether I had conceived her or carried her, it does not seem to matter to my maternal instincts. It is time to nest. I start scrubbing bathrooms, then mop the floor, I load the washing machine and polish wood furniture. I organize her pink clothes and make space for her in the kitchen and the bedroom. An elaborate diaper changing area appears and a basket with bottle fixins takes prominence in the kitchen. Our honored guest will get all the special treatment she deserves.

Of course, while scrubbing, mopping, folding and polishing, my mind is busier than my hands worrying about that baby's mama. The questions buzzing in my head might be the most difficult part to deal with. Can Katy survive this? I KNOW this woman and her spirit and feel very strongly that Katy can tackle any obstacle. But this was no simple detour and that lump in the ICU bed, she wasn't exactly Katy. My heart aches for her and her new baby girl.

Amid my cleaning, sorting, scrubbing and worrying, I start remembering what it was like to be a new mother. The happiest day of my life. Samuel was perfect and healthy with a hearty appetite and a sweet disposition. An instant thumb sucker and the greatest joy of my life. It's a mother's job to note all the little details of their baby, the minutiae of their life, especially the beginning. How will Katy know her baby? Who will tell Arielle the story of her first car ride, first trip to the ER, first sleepover? Katy can. I smile as a simple solution takes hold in my imagination. I'll keep a journal for Katy, of Arielle's every day, and Katy will know. She'll know how much Arielle was cared for and Katy won't miss out entirely. Arielle can look back on these notes and read about these precious memories. I'll journal. My gift to Katy and Arielle. I'll start today.

It's very late and I survey my clean house as the phone rings unexpectedly. After the initial shock of an 11:30 pm phone call, I frown with worry as my stomach tightens with dread. The call is from Al and I am ashamed of my reaction. Is she dead? Don't think like that! And yet, that is the question on my heart and the worry in my fingers as I reach to answer the phone. There is no change in Katy's condition. Al is checking in with me about his daughter. We agree to talk daily and he promises to try and sneak away for a visit soon.

This is how it all began. A rare illness, a victim with the heart of a champion, a little pink baby and me.

Our first night together

Arielle, you are only five days old. Yesterday your mother, my dear friend, went into the hospital. Today, she is fighting for her life. We do not know what the future holds. But you my dear are the most wonderful thing in this situation. Please know that every detail of your life is gloriously important and cherished.

I saw a Facebook post that Katy was in the hospital. I called Al immediately and asked what I could do. He asked me if I could go get the baby (that's you). You were at home, sleeping in Grandpa Ike's arms. I was your first car ride. I had to find the car seat in the garage and get it all together. My son Sam and nanny-boy Kendrick were home from school that President's Day ~ they were excited to have you come home and play with them. I had to take you up to the hospital (Kingwood Medical Center) twice so they could test you and make sure you didn't have the Strep A your Mama was fighting.

Your umbilical stump is quite smelly so I'm cleaning it twice a day. Today is so confusing, lots of upheaval. You are a handsy baby with long delicate fingers and lovely oval nails. A good crop of dark hair and dark gray eyes. You get the hiccups a lot and I am reminded that this happened when you were still in your Mama's belly too. I saw your Mama in the ICU. I have met lots of family ~ they all rushed here for support. Our Mom's Group, MOYC (Mother's of Young Children) have descended upon us and provided everything, meeting all our needs.

So much excitement and adrenaline makes it hard to sleep. I start nesting too.

Overnight, the hottest topic in my household is milk. Breast milk to be exact. Katy wanted to nurse baby Arielle and now we're scrambling to determine the best course of action. Babies need to eat, a lot, and the milk machine is out of commission. The family had started giving her formula. When I picked up Arielle the day before, I grabbed the only bottle I could find. Turns out, it was the only bottle they had and we never could find the cap. One opened tub of formula was on the counter which I packed away for mealtime. It seems Grandpa Ike had fed her earlier and then expressed his dissatisfaction with formula and confessed to giving her plain water.

I know some core Moms in our tight-knit community and reach out to them and their lactating friends. How would they feel about sharing any extra breast milk? Suzanne is the local lactation expert and she walks me through some of the screening, testing and handling that is done for the protection of the baby. All this information is weighing me down as we consider that the nearest breast milk bank is four hours away in Austin. Could we gather enough independent providers? The challenge with that, other than the ethical and non-tested concerns, was that each individual would be providing milk unique to them and their diet. So if we had milk from Mom A for breakfast and Mom B for lunch and Mom C for dinner....you see the problem. There is also forced lactation for mothers who want to nurse. I look down at my chest, once productive and useful for satisfying my own child's nutritional needs. I knew my diet and health and could provide a consistent source. I wondered what my 41 year old breasts would look like after that? Not exactly a plus in the dating world. Am I being selfish? Were there limits to what I would do for my friend? Is this even an option they would be comfortable considering?

I fill a bottle with hot tap water and drop in two scoops of powder. Screw on the cap and shake it until it's "milk". Pop into screaming mouth. Ah. Sometimes the obvious solution, is the best solution.

All this is shared with Al. Whatever Daddy wants, I try to make happen. But I caution him with this detail, everyone involved is already working to capacity. The simpler we keep this, the more likely it is we can provide his infant with some badly needed consistency. Anyone can make her bottle after bottle with similar results. Al and I converse earnestly about the milk topic. It is a conversation most new parents share, oftentimes, if there has been a breastfeeding issue. But I'm willing to wager, few people have this conversation while Mom lies unconscious, unaware of her baby's milk fate. At no time does Al belittle my milk concerns and I appreciate his attention to this detail. Maybe it is even a bit of a re-prieve for him to talk about breast milk vs. bottles and step a few feet away from the tubes and machines sustaining his wife's very breath and virtually every organ.

We decide to stick with formula. Once this decision is known, the heavens open up and angels from Kingwood United Methodist Church (KUMC), led by Whitney, show up with formula and bottles, enough to feed Arielle for the first year of her life. The Young Mom's Bible study quickly becomes part of our "team" that we rely upon to manage this one-of-a-kind situation. Their generosity does not end with for-mula and includes clothing, monogrammed goodies, toys, diapers, wipes and everything else under the sun. What a comfort it is to know that I will not be alone on this journey.

**Arielle, Aunt Betta
and Al**

Uncle Tom

Someone brought us a pretty, white bassinet. I put it upstairs with me. I've been living in the guest room to be closer to Sam and now the three of us are upstairs. The weather is quite chilly but it's nice and warm for us. You also have a giraffe-print, pillow sleeper to sleep in and a pink, oval bouncy-type thing that vibrates.

Feeding you formula but trying to find a source of breast milk. The midwife, Alice, insists on Nestle Good Start formula. I'm using an Avent bottle. You're a good eater. I run a humidifier all the time to combat dryness and it makes a nice, white noise.

I sing to you a lot. Today, it was mostly Beatles songs with a smattering of lullabies. I'm exhausted already.

A small group of thoughtful people could change the world. Indeed, it's the only thing that ever has.
Margaret Mead

My phone never stops ringing with calls from concerned friends desperate for a word of hope, news of Arielle and Katy and offers of help. No real news on Katy as she continues her battle with Strep A. I am completely overwhelmed with the constant barrage of calls, questions and concerns. To manage the mayhem, I start to compartmentalize. The baby. My new phrase excuses me from any real medical knowledge or other duties and announces that "I've got the baby."

Our mutual friend and my trusted bestie, Britt, generates Care Calendars for my little family with needs slotted and needs filled. Within hours an army of men and women piece together a plan, descend upon the Hayes household and implement heroic acts of kindness, generosity and selfless love. Five-year-old Jake, Al and Katy's son, has gone to live with a nearby friend in his school district. Jake's school, notified of the situation will provide him with free school lunches. Someone cleans their home. That first day, when I pick up the baby, there was the normal mess but signs of something wrong too. Like the chair and tray that had upturned and lay dramatically on the floor. Someone has volunteered and picked that up. Amber spends a lot of time at the hospital and I know she is missing some school. Can you blame her? She and Katy are so close. The three dogs need care too. Amber is home for feedings but someone, one of these many friends or neighbors, picks up the dog poop. These are the details of our lives we don't consider when contracting a deadly disease. Who takes care of that?

We will. Or I should say "they will". I have the baby and she is all I can handle. I say "all" but maybe I should say she's maxed me out. My son, I smile just thinking about his kind and generous spirit, welcomes baby Arielle into our home with such an open heart. He is at school until 3:15 p.m. and Arielle and I usually sleep most of that time in preparation for our endless nights of screaming and discontent. So far we are managing to keep to our schedule and Sam relishes the opportunity to help with the new baby.

My dear you are one week old! We're so glad you're here! We love having you in our lives.

Today you had professional pictures taken of you by Gia. She had you on a heating pad and a blanket by the window and spent two hours cuddling and photographing your smile, your toes, your hair, your fingers, your everything!

You love having your face touched.

Al and Betta come over late and visit you. I have the lights low and light candles trying to make it a calm and pleasant sanctuary from the harsh atmosphere of the ICU.

Last night I got 2 1/2 hours of sleep. I am deliriously tired. Your umbilical stump fell off today in time for your photo shoot. Church tonight.

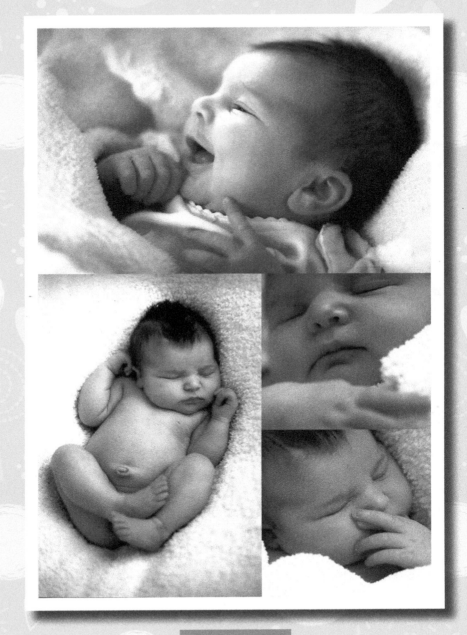

1 week old

You scream a lot at night. It makes our mornings difficult. I'm trying a variety of tricks but nothing seems to soothe you. You do fine all day, eating, interacting, sleeping. But at night, eegad!

Me "Sam, what have you learned about having a new baby in the house?" Sam "Well, she's kinda wrinkly, she takes a lot of work, but she's really cute".

I am becoming so sleep-deprived I'm forgetting things. People keep offering to help so I can go to the gym or the grocery store. All I want to do is go back to bed.

I'm in love. My heart swells with sweet feelings for this new baby in my arms. How will you ever give her up? These seven words haunt me. She is not mine to keep but simply to care for. As a single mother of a young son, swaddling a little pink baby with ease, we probably look like the perfect family. We three smile, we sing, we interact and baby has become an integral part of our lives. Yes, a guest at first, but so much more. It is impossible to care so completely without losing your heart. Part of that care, is the love that you know is supposed to be bestowed upon a new life. My son had every advantage. She should too. Baby Arielle will receive the very best care I can provide. Love included.

But what does "giving her up" mean? Giving her back to her loving parents seems a relatively natural thing to hope for and happen. Her mother's condition continues to be exceedingly desperate. Every hour Katy clings to life defies the odds. There is no good news. Survival should be enough but it barely seems to be an option. I don't think the hospital staff expected her to live through the first night much less four days. Her condition poses other scenarios. With Al posted by Katy's side, he is taking on the immeasurable task of fighting for her very being. Is he strong enough for both of them? In my heart, I know Katy is stronger than we think, but this is beyond reason. If we are optimists, Katy lives. Our daily hope is that she regains consciousness. With Katy and Al out of this picture, Baby Arielle is mine for now. I guess the answer lies in whether Katy lives or dies. Even more sickening, how long she is in the hospital or how quickly she dies.

These bleak thoughts bring such sadness over the joy of a healthy new baby girl. Although difficult, I do my best to keep my focus on my priorities. My wonderful son, our pink houseguest, my sleep and wellbeing are vitally important. The stress of Katy's critical situation, the baby's own mother, takes a backseat if I am to continue doing what I need to do. So we don't talk about giving her up. And we don't talk about Katy dying. We sing lullabies and tell Arielle she is loved by her wonderful mother Katy, her sweet Daddy Al, her sister Amber, her brother Jake and the fact that right now, at this moment, she is loved by me too.

The winter weather is drying out your skin and your feet are peeling. I give you a bath every morning ~ you <u>LOVE</u> your bath. After you're all clean, I use a little baby lotion and give you baby massage. Your Mom taught me how to do this. Your Mom has magic hands and I'm trying to use my hands to put all the love back in you. Katy would do this for you. I will try my best. I tell you what each move is and talk about your body. Not your favorite activity.

You go home to visit your family tonight for two hours getting used to smells, pets and people.

Alice, the midwife, shows up just before midnight. She swaddles you, gives you a pacifier and you both sleep on the sofa. I crawl off to bed to get some well-deserved and desperately-needed sleep.

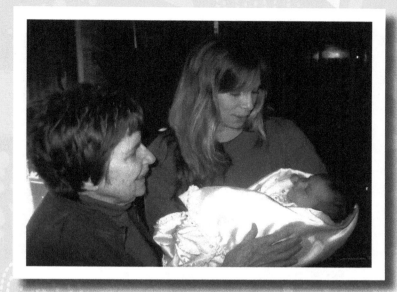

**Grandma Lucy and
Aunt Jennifer**

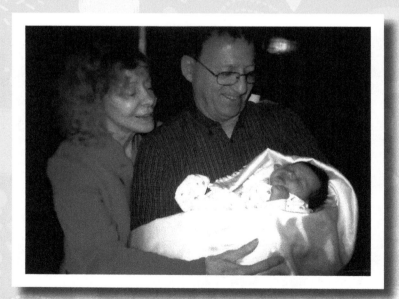

**Nona (Tina) and
Nono (Ike)**

Grandpa Bill and
Grandma Pat

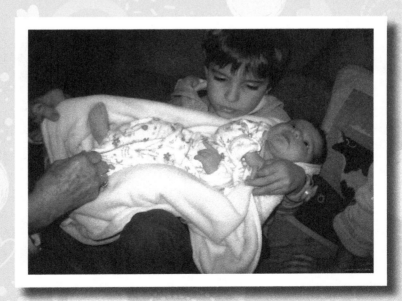

Big brother Jake

This Saturday, Cassandra came over to sit with you so I could go to yoga. I really needed that. Then my church friend Dawna came over so I could go up to the hospital and see your Mommy. I went with my friend Britt. I touched your Mom and joked with her. Her nurse had braided her hair. I told her about you, her precious girl.

When I change your diaper, you grab my hand with your feet.

When did it happen? I am completely in love with you. I adore you and have taken you fully and completely into my heart and my life. You are welcome as long as you like.

I hurt all over. My neck and shoulders are tense from stress and carrying Arielle so much and pain is settling in my low back too. I desperately need a massage but the thought alone plagues me with gut-wrenching guilt. Katy is my massage therapist and has been so for several years. She's amazing! I wouldn't even know where to begin to look for someone new. But if this stress brings me down, how will I take care of my responsibilities? So many people are relying on me. Deep breath. A friend finds someone willing to come to my house and I schedule a secretive meeting. I make sure no one is around and schedule it during Arielle's nap time. The "professional", a man no less, arrives and I sneak him in as though hiding a fugitive. "No one can know" I think to myself plagued with disloyalty to my Katy. But as I lay on the table, tense and stressed and anxious for some relief, Arielle starts crying. My masseur Will, scoops up the baby and deftly juggles that inconsolable, colicky girl and massages me one-handed the entire hour. Will's skills as a massage therapist do wonders for my stress but the mere fact he's holding that crying baby for me, comforting us both, is a gift. In my heart, Katy will always be my massage therapist. But until her return, I will continue to seek the many benefits massage brings to me.

A lazy Sunday morning. We never made it to church. My friend Renee called. Her husband, Kris, is German and they have a tradition of sharing coffee and pastries with new Moms. We welcomed them with open arms. Megan joined us too.

They give your Mom an experimental Vitamin C therapy which generates positive results.

You are very alert and love lights. You have a strong neck too. I sing to you often.

This is a wonderful, blessed time we are sharing.

Al (your Daddy) has a plan to get you back home. We talk about it and agree, but then I have some concerns, Daddy does too. It is agreed that <u>one</u>, consistent caregiver is vital. I am honored.

2 1/2 hours of sleep last night. You sleep in my room – well, you're supposed to sleep in my room but you have been crying and screaming uncontrollably. I'm so exhausted I'm afraid to drive Sam to school. Back to bed.

Renee brought egg salad for lunch. Yum.

2:20 p.m. We get a phone call from Lettie with Channel 39. 4:00 p.m. she interviews you and I for an hour. 9:10 p.m. the news airs and you, my darling, are a TV star.

I am so excited with how well it went I go to sleep late.

You have adorable toes. They're long and skinny and your big toe has a joint in it. I kiss your toes a lot and play with your feet.

Al is researching options for Katy online and it looks like a Burn Unit with a hyperbaric chamber and specialized treatment options that could help regenerate skin tissue are her only hope. Katy has at least two black patches on her skin that I have seen. The most obvious is a finger pad on her left hand that is black and wrinkled like an aged grape. Is this what frostbite looks like? This dead tissue is a result of her Strep A morphing into a form of necrotizing fasciitis, also known as flesh-eating disease. She also has a black toe. Is there more? Al is holding off on making the decision as to whether to amputate these affected areas. Everyone is so concerned about this development and we watch it closely. If it gets worse, then the unimaginable must happen. But Al believes there is a chance she can recover fully. We cling to this hope but the days tick away with no real response from Katy and our worries only increase.

Al is taking Katy to Dallas and they are leaving soon. Nothing seems to happen for days and then a whirlwind of craziness is decided and we all hold on for dear life. However inconceivable, there isn't an available Burn Unit bed in the Houston area for Katy. So Al is Life Flight-ing her to Dallas' Parkland Hospital. With Al basically living at the hospital he ventures home to shower and say good night to his son Jake. Al's sister Betta is with the kids for now. With Al so far away this creates additional changes, especially for Baby Arielle. A few phone calls, some tough questions, all my secret information and I now have Medical Power of Attorney over Arielle. What a strange feeling. Kind of important and surreal and daunting. I carefully safeguard these two folded documents tucked on the designated top shelf with all her pink things.

You like having your hands near your face. Yes, you've scratched your face already. I file your nails but they are so new they tend to slough off before I get to them. You like to have a hand on or near the bottle at feeding time and today you held my finger while I fed you.

I have been trying too hard to please others. You and I need a better plan. I'm putting you on the <u>Baby Wise</u> schedule. I will wake you every three hours for a bottle. During the day you'll eat and interact before going back to sleep. At night, it will be a survival feeding. Bottle and bed. Let's try this out sister.

Your Dad is taking your Mom to Dallas. They arrange to give me Medical Power of Attorney for you while you are in my care. It's a big deal.

Al and Arielle

These are my sleep-deprived ramblings. There is no reason to the stream of consciousness that my muddled brain fabricates. I don't remember being this exhausted with Sam. But I had different help. With the birth of my son I had a husband and constant family help, mostly my mother. And Sam was the easiest baby ever, I truly don't remember him crying or fussing.

I'm too tired to drive in the afternoons. Noel drives me to the bank because I am so exhausted I'm walking around with only one eye open. At the bank drive-through, the clerk calls my name. "How is Katy?" Even the bank tellers know that Katy and I are friends and hope that today I might have some good news to share. I turn my head and with one eye open, I confirm she's still holding on. "And the baby?" The baby, the baby that doesn't sleep. I smile. "She's great!"

And what "am" I through all this? We've kind of crossed the traditional friend boundary at this point. For cryin' out loud I know Katy's urine output, and her daughter's for that matter. Maybe I should call myself her Advocate. Defined as "someone who speaks on behalf of another person" I embrace this new title. Of course, like all things in life, this situation and my duties continually evolve. I then decide to look up the definition of Ambassador. This one says "highly respected individuals, assigned specific responsibilities, working to advise and assist". Either way, our bond has not been tested in the least, only pointed in a new direction.

Sydney brought us Pei Wei for lunch. Yum! They (MOYC-Care Calendar) has arranged mealtime visits. It is the highlight of my day. They help a little with you, bring me food and we have grown-up time. Of course we mostly just talk about you and your Mom. You represent hope and all things good. Katy is such a warm, good friend to so many of us. We are all praying for your Mama and for you.

You have lots of visitors today. Daddy Bill, Aunt Betta, Grandma Pat and Amber came over for some quality time. Amber is frustrated and questions why the baby is with me. They bring me the changing table. This is the beginning of me converting my office into your nursery, your new room. You are two weeks old! :) Church tonight.

It is rare to meet your girlfriend's entire family and match up all the stories to the faces. There are so many people touching my life so graciously during these days. Katy's dad is Daddy Bill and he provides a strong male figure while Al is away. His girlfriend, yes, girlfriend, we call Grandma Pat. Grandma Pat is a smile and a hug and a home cooked meal. She starts family dinners again and begins to take over duties that the Care Calendar folks have been handling. Daddy Bill and Grandma Pat weren't here at the beginning but came in as the second wave. Daddy Bill is a bit crotchety and he's a mess over his middle daughter, dealing with his anguish in his own gruff ways. He is quick to offer to help with the baby and happy to sit in the same house as his grandchild. He's less enthused about diapering or feeding. My plans better have me back before a fresh diaper is necessary. He comes over and sits with Arielle one morning while I run errands and have lunch with Sam. Once a week lunches with Sam are a highlight and something I've done with him since kindergarten. Now they often occur with baby in tow. Grandma Pat dotes too but in a more neutral way. She always has a kind word and compliment for me. It touches my heart and makes me miss my Mom. My mother is alive and well in Oklahoma City but angered at me over a phone call and hasn't spoken to me in nine months. She would be a big help. Mom's do the stuff that need to be done without asking. Now I have neither a mother or a husband. But I am not alone and grateful for this amazing opportunity to touch and be touched by so many. Grateful and humbled by this odd assortment of someone else's family, friends and complete strangers filled with compassion as they support us through a helpless situation spanning a maze of medical dismay and perfect pink baby girl moments.

Daddy Bill came over this morning to sit with you so I can go to the bank and the grocery store. I taught him about diapers before I left.

Lisa brought lunch in a glamorous, retro picnic basket. It was yummy too!

I work on setting up the nursery and organizing the truckloads of donations that church groups (KUMC-Kingwood United Methodist Church Young Mom's Bible Study ~ Whitney), MOYC, friends, neighbors and strangers bring.

Your screaming tonight is so bad I call Noel and she brings Mylicon drops and takes a shift with you. I think Mylicon helps a little. Your tummy seems unhappy.

I will forever think of a "bad day" in different terms. Today is a very bad day indeed. The black on Katy's finger and toe, which has stayed small for so long, has spread rapidly and she is losing her battle. Her only hope now is amputation. My heart breaks for Al, making these heartbreaking decisions.

Arielle is having "family time" during the weekdays and I drop her off now in the late afternoon for a couple of hours. Al wants to make sure Arielle is accustom to the smells and noises of her real life. When I pick her up this evening, everything is all wrong. The house is full of people but it's too quiet and their faces register a sort of shell-shocked, dazed look. Everyone is avoiding eye contact and when they finally look up, their red-rimmed eyes show the misery their insides must feel. This is how I learn of Katy's lessening. Off with the bad so the good can continue fighting. I have no idea how to deal with this development and tears seem a very reasonable response. My Dad in Michigan answers my phone call and listens to me unload my heartbreak and horror over it all. He understands my frustration and my sense of helplessness and everything feeling out of control. When I journal, I try to be sensitive about this day specifically. Katy has yet to regain consciousness and we all wonder if she will even survive the operations. Disease has robbed her of her flesh and now amputation is the only option.

Katy loses all four limbs above the joint.

I love Katy and she is an amazing, warm and giving person. Wednesday they life-flighted her to Dallas for additional treatment options at Parkland Hospital. The news today is sad. Your mother will be a different mother than others. It frustrates me to think of what Katy <u>won't</u> be able to do. Here I list some things she <u>will</u> be able to do:

see you grow up
smile
say loving, encouraging things
laugh
blow bubbles
sing
blow kisses
tongue Olympics
scream
bite
make silly faces
spit watermelon seeds

I picked you up at home, you were having family time and Daddy Bill hugged me like he was a drowning man. I cried on the way home.

Last night Jane brought her girls over and we had dinner. Yummy.

This was our morning to meet the doctor and get you all checked out. Dr. Boyd called in a favor to get us seen so quickly. Sam is at a play date with Evan and you and I are off to meet your new pediatrician, Dr. Smith. I'm rather concerned you have thrush and you spit-up an unseemly amount. Exam goes well but he's concerned about your weight and switches you to soy formula. Soy formula trial begins.

This morning at breakfast, Sam keeps touching your forehead. I asked him what he was doing. "I'm baptizing her." he replied.

The three of us go to church. Sam is singing this morning. Many in the congregation are surprised to see me toting a newborn. Many tears are shed for you and your Mom. (By the way, the Monday I picked you up, I called my church and put your Mom on our Prayer list.) Sermon is about mothers.

Grampy (my step-Dad) comes to visit that afternoon. Karen from church brings us chicken and noodles and applesauce. Larry baked us homemade bread. Belle made red Jell-O with marshmallows. It's a beautiful day and we all take a walk. Amber and her Dad come over to see you and walk with us.

The soy doesn't seem different than the other formula but your poop went from yellow diarrhea to clay.

With a slew of help, it takes six hours to sort through donations. Some are returned, some set for resale, some garage sale, some for now, some for later, some you've already outgrown.

I feel like a Mommy detective. Navigating the formula nuances. Tricks to quiet your screams. Relief for your belly, your burps, your incessant hiccups. I want the best for you.

The quickest way to soothe you is to let you suck my pinkie. I just turn my little finger upside down and you are quite content.

Noel and Cam with Arielle

Last night you slept six hours. Everyone asked if I was worried about you. Girl, I was <u>asleep</u>. Thank you! If this is the soy, I'm a believer.

We girls run errands this morning including a stop at church. Karen holds you as they all ooh and aah over your pinkness. You are a <u>beautiful</u> baby. You have such pretty, delicate features. Your heart-shaped face and dark hair make you unforgettable.

Ever since you've arrived, everyone asks how long you will stay. I do not have the answer. Your Mom needs constant care right now. The various family is busy just taking care of Jake, Amber, three dogs, cat, parakeets, groceries, cooking, cleaning, hospital calls/visits and life plans. I have Sam and the two black labs (Clive and Nixon). I can take care of you. I will take care of you as long as need be. Your Dad and I talk almost every single night. He really loves your Mom and is doing everything he can for her. I tell him all about you, his baby girl.

Grandma Pat, Amber and Daddy Bill all take shifts with you tonight. I went to the rodeo to see Dierks Bently in concert. Good times.

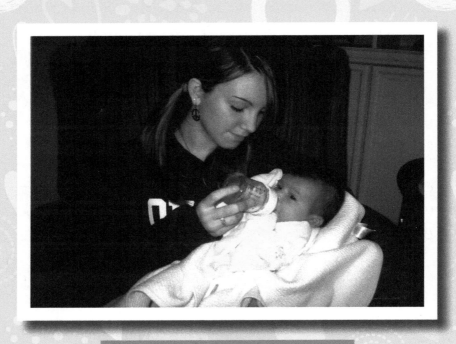

Big sister Amber with Arielle

Katy and I first met when she was working as a massage therapist at a local spa. Then, she and Al ran into me where I was working as a teaching Chef. I loved their smiles and their energy. Shortly after that, I hired Katy to come do a Girl's Night slumber party I was hosting. She was a hit at the party and we all lined up for our fifteen minutes of pampering massage. Thus began our business relationship.

However, your massage therapist is a lot like your bartender, your hairdresser and your shrink combined. You work it all out on that table. Katy and I learned quickly that we had a lot in common. We are exactly ten days apart in age, we both grew up in Michigan and we have many common interests and goals like family and gardening and yoga. Over the years I have followed Katy from one office to another until she set up shop in her house.

When I first met Katy she, Al and Amber were living in a two-bedroom apartment not far from my house in Bear Branch with their two dogs, Angel and Roddy, a cat named Chyna and a parrot named Miranda. I know when Miranda escaped during their last move, she searched for her endlessly and cried over her loss.

I helped Katy locate a space in a hair studio for her nail and massage business and made her homemade scones for her grand opening. She always accidentally called them sconces so we joked that I had brought pastries to "illuminate" her clients.

For my fortieth birthday Al and Katy presented me with a beautiful purple vase filled with lovely, fresh flowers Katy had arranged for me. It was thoughtful and appreciated!

She and Al liked going down to Surfside Beach hanging out, drinking a cold beer or splashing in the waves, playing music together and watching the kids enjoy the outdoors.

Katy wanted a baby so badly. A baby with Al. And their son Jake was a dream come true. The arrival of Jake meant another move to a bigger place and Katy finally moved her business home. This arrangement allowed her to work and parent simultaneously. Truly, the best of both worlds.

Katy joined my Mom's group and became a valuable force. Katy and Al grabbed the reins of the Friday Create and Play playgroup. When I became President, Katy stepped up as VP and when I stepped down, Katy, secretly pregnant with Arielle, became President. This group, Mother's of Young Children, would provide the backbone of support through Katy's crisis.

Katy and Al enjoyed going to Rock, Wine and Blues in Atascocita and listening to live music and sometimes Al would jam with the band.

Tin Roof BBQ was another of Katy's favorite spots that is really kid-friendly and had karaoke nights.

Katy enjoyed working out and exercising. She was so active. At Gold's Gym she loved taking Body Pump and Studio Cycle and Body Combat.

Another passion and creative outlet was making beaded jewelry. She loved working with her hands and she and her friend Kayla made necklaces, earrings and bracelets. I still have the set she made me for Christmas one year.

Katy was generous and caring to an extreme. When struggling with infertility and beginning my journey with invitro-fertilization,

Local women's group provides support, encouragement to mothers

Mother's of Young Children is a local group of amazing women. With "Mothers Helping Mothers" as their motto, these ladies are making the community a better place for children.

Monthly meetings give ladies a great excuse for two hours of "adult" time. Moms sharing similar experiences can share ideas and gain perspective in a relaxed, non-denominational group setting that is casual. Speakers at the meetings are excited about their topics and involve the audience with questions and practical applications on topics ranging from home improvement to recycling to nutrition or a spa day.

Friendships made in MOYC last longer than a child's clean room. Offering Bunco groups, supper club, age-specific playgroups and Create and Play for all ages MOYC has much to offer. People new to the community and new to parenthood are especially encouraged to try an MOYC meeting.

The MOYC digital newsletter is a wealth of parental knowledge. See what's going on and who is doing what. Mom tips and recipes round out this monthly e-mail.

Member-only parties for kids are the top-rated kids' events in the community.

The Mothers of Young Children board members are, from left on the back row, Katy Hayes, Create and Play Group; Rhonda Schnitz, membership; Michele Dykstra, programs director; Erin Messersmith, vice president; Karen Tartamella, communications; middle row, Paula Tobey, president; seated, Jane Carter, publicity; and Shea Maness, secretary.

Offered three times a year, children are sure to delight in MOYC's Fall Fest, Breakfast with Santa and Spring Fling.

MOYC also gives back to the community. March of Dimes is one of their more prominent beneficiaries. MOYC Moms donate time and money to save babies together.

One of the many benefits MOYC offers its members is the Meals for Moms program.

Meals are lovingly provided to mothers of newborns and those in need.

MOYC meets the third Thursday of the month during the school year. Fun meetings from 7:30 p.m. last until 9 p.m. and are located at Holy Comforter Lutheran Church on Woodland Hills. Check out their Web site at *www.kingwoodmoyc.org* for additional information.

monthly massages were part of the plan. The medical process was both painful and stressful on me. Katy would mix special essential oils and pampered me through my pregnancy and continued with remedying my new Mom aches. My arms, neck and shoulders were so sore from incessant holding and carrying of my solid son. As my marriage crumbled around me, Katy not only hugged me, listened to me and massaged away my stresses, she filled me with love. She was patient, she'd work longer than I paid, she would spot when if I had no money, she was a true friend to me.

Katy planted a giant vegetable garden and took such pride in growing good, nutritious food for her family.

She and Al had plans and dreams to travel. They enjoyed camping and liked to visit the Austin area. Katy liked to eat dinner down the road at Skeeter's and drink margaritas at Sharky's by the river.

She wore reading glasses and smelled like patchouli. That smell would have a Pavlovian effect on me whenever we would hug. We might run into each other at Gold's Gym and hug and I'd just sigh and think "Ah. It's Katy."

Al's work required he travel extensively and often Katy felt like a single Mom holding down the fort, managing the kids and working full-time. The sharing went both ways and I can recount Katy sharing arguments and miscommunications between her and Al. She also told me their love story, how they met, their courtship, their wedding. Two dreamers with big ideas and a lust for life.

Amber, Al and Arielle

This morning I am rushing to get us both ready. Jennifer from The Observer newspaper is coming at 9:30 a.m. to interview us about your Mom. She wanted to get to know more about your Mom as a person. We shared tidbits and plenty of stories. They have said the article should make the front page.

Skeeter's restaurant is hosting a fundraiser tonight for your Mom. It is a huge success! Not only is it the 2nd largest fundraiser they've ever had, the line was crazy long, bringing the community closer. Mary Kay was bringing me dinner and didn't arrive with my Southwest Salad until 9 p.m. Michelle had stopped by for a few to calm you. Then Mary Kay had a turn.

A very busy day for the ladies. Sam will be gone this weekend so we join him for lunch. We bring him a meatball sub from Subway and goodies from home. Then off to HCLC (that's my church) for The Gathering Place. I teach five minutes of yoga and stay for lunch while you sleep peacefully. Next we head to the Atascocita office of Humble Pediatrics to follow-up with Dr. Smith. He gives us A+s. No allergies, great weight gain, we do a heel prick and head out. On the way home I celebrate this victory with ice cream from Marble Slab. :) Cindy brings Pei Wei for dinner and stays late. We have heartfelt talks about you, your Mom, this situation and life in general. Krystal stops by with late night donations and makes us laugh. My mother calls (we've been estranged 9 months) and will be here Monday to help with you. Oh my.

I'm worried that your Mom might resent me. Actually, I wonder if she'll hate me. This is a deep topic with many challenges. From my heart, I'm trying to give you all the love she would have given you. Let my hands be a tool, by proxy, of love.

No Sam this weekend but <u>WE</u> slept in. It's a gorgeous day and I introduced you to my neighbors, Pam and Hal.

I love spending time with you. What do I call myself? I am mothering you but I also know your Mama and that she is working hard to get back to you. Miss Michele seems a bit formal. Mama Michele? We'll work it out.

Lazy morning. We slept in again. Missed church. Gorgeous outside. Is Spring nearing?

Dottie from church came and sat with you so I could run up to the gym and work off some stress. As I enter Gold's Gym, there is a donation envelope with your Mom's pictures and story. I got choked up. She worked out a lot. Her friend Kayla works at Gold's and they make jewelry together.

Gripewater in your bottle – OUR FIRST QUIET NIGHT! Thank God!

82nd Academy Awards, Sandra Bullock wins and thanks those who raise others children and I sobbed.

Excerpted from Sandra Bullocks' acceptance speech for winning Best Actress in The Blind Side at the 82nd Academy awards.

"Not enough time, so I would like to thank what this film is about for me which are the moms that take care of the babies and the children no matter where they come from. Those moms and parents never get thanked. Thank you."

Sandra Bullock

Sam dotes on you. He checks on you first thing, insists on kissing you and sings you songs. It can be quite a struggle to get the three of us up and going ~ especially on school days.

As much as you <u>love</u> your bath and tolerate the lotion massage, you <u>hate</u> having clothes pulled over your head. Whether on or off, you always voice your displeasure.

When did your eyes turn dark blue? Just lovely. Trying Gripewater in your bottle in the evenings and it seems to be helping. You're sleeping now and I'm busy doing laundry, dishes, packing lunches, writing in your journal, catching up with friends.

Sam feeds the baby

We slept all morning. In the afternoon I get you all gussied up for errands. First stop, Vitamins and Such, where Amrita and everybody holds and dotes on you. Amrita tells me she saw your Mom the Saturday after you were born and was extremely concerned about her pain and the way she looked. Amrita is vocal about her concerns. She is also emotional and tearful over how wonderful you are.

Tonight, Cassandra comes over to sit with you. Sam, Grandma and I, go out for Mexican food. Sam adores you but you take a ton of our energy. I don't want him to resent you or become jealous so we've arranged some help so Sam gets one-on-one time too.

Your ears are a little fuzzy. Time to trim your nails again. Decided to keep you on soy formula. :)

The KUMC Young Mom's Bible Group has been such a blessing. They show up regularly and it's like Christmas. I wanted to personally thank these amazing women. I didn't tell them we were coming ~ it's hard to tell if we'll get up and going at a reasonable hour. (We were up from 3:30–5:00 a.m.). However, we wheeled into their meeting all cute and clean. There were probably 80 women there and I recognized several faces. Most of the women cried when we came. They lined up to hug me and hold you. They prayed for us and for your entire family. It was very moving. People kept handing me money for you too.

Beautiful, sunny, 80°F day. Busy and productive.

1 month old

DIVERSIONS
HAAM celebrates its
new resale shop. See
page **1B**

GHW
Houston celebrates St.
Patrick's Day with
parades and pub events

PASTA HARVEST
ALL YOU CAN EAT
PASTA & SALAD
only $8.99
Carino's
ITALIAN

T★ KINGWOOD ★
HE OBSERVER

WEDNESDAY

Find the latest local news, sports and more at www.thekingwoodobserver.com

MARCH 10, 2010 ■ Vol. 33, No. 10

Local mother fights for life, community rallies support

By JENNIFER SUMMER
jsummer@hcnonline.com

As a very down-to-earth person, she often smelled of soils and nature. Katy Hayes and her husband, Al, are a non-traditional couple who are very active and "green," as they built a gazebo and a vegetable garden in their back yard.

Katy has always been willing to step forward to help her friends and family, but now she is in need of help from the community.

"The Hayes family has always been very active. I met Katy eight years ago through Mothers of Young Children. Katy's personality and great smile is always very welcoming," Michele Dykstra, a close family friend of the Hayes, said.

Both self-employed, Al, a musician, and Katy, a massage therapist, were very excited about the arrival of their two children - Amber, 16, and Jake, 5.

After she gave birth to her almost-10-pound daughter, Arielle, at home through a midwife, she began to experience severe pain, and the 41-year-old mother checked into Kingwood Medical Center. She was then transferred to a medical center in Dallas where she is now battling for life due to complications resulting from a

See HAYES, Page 4A

Streptococcal A infection.

She has experienced multiple organ failure, has had several sepsis organs removed, part of her colon, portions of her extremities such as the portions just above the elbows of both arms and portions of her legs, and is currently on a ventilator and undergoing dialysis.

"Al has been by her side the whole time and they are both strong people, so I know they will pull through this. Since this has happened, Al has shared everything that is happening through his blog. It makes you realize that if you love someone, you should tell them everyday," Dykstra said.

Since Al is staying by Katy's side until she recovers, Dykstra is the caregiver for Arielle and has kept a journal so Katy and Al know what happened in the first couple of weeks in Arielle's life.

Kingwood resident Paula Tobey has known Katy for seven years and has partnered with several other community members to start fundraising and collecting donation items for the Hayes family.

Tobey and Dykstra are past presidents of Mothers of Young Children, which Katy was the president of before she fell ill.

"Katy has helped MOYC be more family-oriented and concentrate on what moms need and what they want. Mothers of Young Children is at its strongest point right now because of Katy's hard work," Tobey said. "Katy's daughter Amber even volunteers to face paint at our Mothers of Young Children events."

Several fundraisers have been set up through the community to help the Hayes family, and a lot of strangers have stepped forward to help Dykstra with Arielle and family in town to help care for the Hayes home and their children. The Hayes family also has growing online support where people can find out more information.

Fundraisers being held include the following:

■ Wednesday, March 10, 6:05 a.m. to 9:05 p.m. Comforter Day at the Kingwood Laundromat, 22401 Loop 494 in Kingwood.

■ Thursday, March 11, 11 a.m. to 10 p.m. A portion of the proceeds from meals purchased at Zammitti's at Kings Harbor, located on Lake Houston Parkway in Kingwood, will go toward the "Help for Katy Hayes" fund.

■ Saturday, March 27, 10 a.m. to 4 p.m. At On the Park Toy Store in Kingwood there will be a Rockin' On Mom-sponsored bake sale.

■ Saturday, April 3, 10 a.m. to 5 p.m. Picnic on the Park "Pink Parlor" in Kingwood Town Center, N. Main Street in Kingwood.

■ Saturday, April 24, 8 a.m. to 4 p.m. Quest High School is sponsoring a garage sale to add their support to the Katy Hayes Fund. All proceeds from the sale will be added to an existing bank account that has been set up for this purpose. The sale will be held on the grounds of Quest's campus on Timber Forest Drive.

■ To make a donation via PayPal, enter KatyHayesFund@yahoo.com or at any Chase Bank branch (account 871725040).

■ Donations of gift cards and baby supplies can be dropped off at Merry-Go-Round on Woodland Hills Drive in Kingwood or Bella Beads on Atascocita Road, the official collection sites for Katy and her family.

To assist the Hayes family in their time of need, Kingwood Mothers of Young Children, www.kingwoodmoyc.org, a local nonprofit organization, is seeking community support.

"They always say it takes a village to raise a child. It is amazing how much the community has stepped forward to help the Hayes family. People who know Katy, Al and the Hayes family are hurting, and helping is their way to heal," Dykstra said.

For more information, log on to www.facebook.com/group.php?gid=343063085090&ref=ts.

Okay sister you're off your schedule! We've also had so many visitors I missed out on a nap. I have implemented a strict bedtime for Grandma and myself to prepare for our upcoming buysness.

Tina (Grandma Nona) has arrived and is anxious to see you. Amber has strep throat (again) so we're postponing a reunion. Betta arrives tomorrow and we'll plan regular visits.

You've had a fussy night but slept peacefully in my arms. Sweet dreams baby girl. :)

Trimmed your nails this afternoon with baby scissors and you screamed emphatically.

Today's visitors: Jeanette (formula and groceries)
                     Liz (lunch)
                     Chef Karen (baby time)
                     Lisa (pet sitting directions)

Zammitti's fundraiser

Sam leaves tonight for nine days. With that in mind (SPRING BREAK) I pull him out of school and head to the rodeo. I dressed you in a onesie with a little footed, fringed, beige outfit that says MY LITTLE COW. It has cow faces on the feet and on the shirt. Grandma Garner handled you most of this trip so Sam could pair with me.

Tonight you were visited by Chris and Faye (from church), Stephanie, Chris, Noel, Onalee and Kendrick.

We're all working to get ready for another big day tomorrow.

Your skin has this perfect glow to it that I try, but fail to capture. You're lovely! :)

Houston Livestock Show & Rodeo 2010

Dallas bound! Okay, we'll be leaving later than expected because we had a HORRIBLE night last night. Tina and Betta coming over for quick visit.

Jeannette's daughter, raised $150. for you last night at her birthday party. For her "gifts" she asked to help you. You've never met. I invited her over for some one-on-one next week.

This "trip" is not going well. After 11:00 a.m. and still not on the road. Betta, Tina and Jake stopped by for a quick pink visit and got a flat tire. Two hours later...

Arrived in Dallas around 5:30 p.m. saw your Mom at 7:00 p.m. We talked about you. Her comments about me caring for you was that I was "So sweet." She loved the pictures I brought of you. Seeing her was VERY difficult for me. I tried to say the right things.

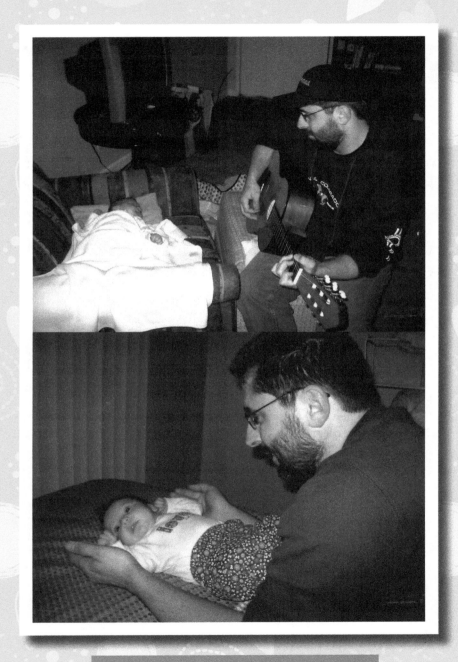

Dallas serenade and quality time

Ever have one of those days where everything seems to go wrong? In an effort to support Al and Katy, we are going to Dallas and we really need to be on the road by 9 am. My visiting Mom, back in my life thanks to baby Arielle, is returning to Oklahoma City and will drop Arielle and I off at Al's Dallas apartment. Al's buddy Chris will drive us home. In fact, Chris dropped his two-seater convertible off at my house Friday night and drove my Jeep to Dallas so that we could all fit comfortably tooling around Dallas and on the ride home. So, like a solider going off to battle, I am packing for every contingency.

I need a good night's rest but unfortunately, Arielle has a rotten night and I fall asleep around 5 a.m. With a long drive to Oklahoma City ahead of her, I let my Mom rest as long as possible. As dawn approaches, I pass Arielle off to her and fall shaking into bed and a deep sleep.

I manage to get up around 9:00 a.m. and am determined to salvage our day even though our schedule is a hot mess. We should be on the road by now. After showering I called Aunt Betta at the Kingwood house. Tina had just popped into town from Austin for a quick stay and was going to miss seeing Arielle. Since we were running behind, I offer to have them stop by for thirty minutes while I get ready and finish with the last minute packing.

But disaster strikes again. As Betta drives Grandma Pat's Michigan mini-van over to my house, she runs over a broken glass bottle and feels the effects instantly as the gashed tire loses air. Neighbor Rick comes to our aid but alas, the spare tire is rusted onto the van and won't come off. Rick and Betta spent the next eight hours together resolving this issue which requires buying an entirely new wheel and tire.

Tina hovers over Arielle but won't pick her up. I keep encouraging her to hold her since she'll be in the car seat for the next four hours. Tina just shakes her head and says she looks content. Jake is bored. With Betta off on the great tire misadventure, Tina decides she and Jake will just hang out at my house until Betta gets back. That's not going to work for me. I'm trying to put on some make-up and get situated and I could not just leave them in my house indefinitely. Once again, Mom to the rescue. She offers to drive them home. With basic directions for the one mile trip, they scoot out the door. I get all ready and finish packing my bag. My mother is still gone. I step outside and look at the pretty day. I double-check some things. I begin to pace. Where is she? Both ways this was a ten-minute journey and she's been gone over half an hour! At last, her loaded white Suburban pulls into the drive with my mother at the wheel shaking her head. It seems that between Jake and Tina they weren't quite sure where the house was and after they found the house, they were locked out. So Tina started crying. Amber was home with Strep throat but didn't hear them ring the doorbell. I'm standing in the driveway listening to my Mother tell me all this and can only join her as I shake my head.

The quick stop at the corner Walgreen's to grab prints of the baby for Katy creates yet another setback. The photos will not be ready for another thirty minutes. These hot-off-the-press pictures are incredibly important and will be all Katy sees of her baby girl. Children are not allowed in the Burn Unit. The baby participation is for Al's sake. But pictures are highly encouraged. It's shortly after noon and if we don't get on the road we're going to miss visitation. And now I'm hungry. Subway sandwiches from across the street provide a tasty lunch but before I can take my first bite,

Arielle fills her britches. Out of the car seat we go, cumbersome diaper bag, baby and I trudge back into Walgreen's and head for the restroom only to be confronted with no diaper changer. Although the back of a Suburban can be spacious, the amount of baby paraphernalia I have packed along with our luggage and my mother's work equipment winds up being a challenge. However, balancing Arielle and her diaper changing pad on top of my suitcase helps me get the job done. With clean pants, washed hands, full bellies and photos in hand. We wearily depart at 1:00 in the afternoon.

My Mom and I head up the feeder road, the same one she has taken hundreds of times on her trips home, laughing at our morning. Then my laughter stops and I just stare at my mother, really stare at her. She missed the exit. The tiniest voice whispers that this trip is doomed and we should just turn around and forget we ever attempted to go to Dallas. As seconds pass my mother realizes her mistake and we start laughing again as she turns around to take the exit. I promptly fall asleep.

Grateful for an easy drive to Dallas improves our outlook and Arielle travels like a superstar. We locate Al's apartment building and a quick call to him reveals he is not at home but still at the hospital. So my anxious-to-get-on-the-road-before-dark mother, the stroller, the baby sleeper/recliner, the diaper bag, Arielle's overnight bag, my overnight bag, a squirmy baby and myself camp out on Al's welcome mat watching the birds cavorting in the bushes near the pool. As amazing as the Kingwood community was for us, the Dallas community heard of Al's plight through another mother's group and step up to help too. He moves out of his scary hotel into this subsidized apartment and local moms cook him meals and bring him groceries. The good that people can do and choose to do for strangers is awe-inspiring.

Al and Chris arrive to greet us and shuffle our caravan of goods inside before my Mom completes her journey. Unpacking and organizing three adults and a baby in a one room space requires a lot of compromise. Somewhat situated and pressed for time we turn around, get back in the car and head to the hospital. The timing of all this is significant. Katy has much shorter and much more controlled visiting hours at Parkland Hospital and Al tries not to miss a minute. His constant vigil has kept her alive. Al has a favorite spot in the parking garage. During non-visiting hours, instead of wasting gas to drive across town to his empty apartment, he often sits in his car and listens to music. We cross the parking lot to the walkway. The elevator doors open with a whir and ding, the bright hallway lights, the sounds of a hospital and scrub- clad people surround us. Up and over we travel to a lobby of sorts for the Burn Unit where people prep before entering. Since Chris has seen Katy, I get to go in with Al first. Special baby blue coverings for our hair, clothes and shoes go on first. Then we wash our hands with a special soap before putting on gloves and a face mask. Will she even be able to recognize me under all this? With all his practice, Al gets ready quickly and urges me along. I walk faster to keep up as we go through the large double doors into the intimate row of rooms.

Taking long strides I reach the nurses station and watch Al walk into Katy's room and then I stop. I just freeze. My heart is pounding. There is no time to waste and yet, standing twenty feet from Katy's door, I am immobilized. Is it fear? Perhaps the thought of meeting Katy, the new Katy, under these circumstances is harder than I imagined. I can't move.

It is as though my feet are cemented in place. I take a deep calming breath of the over-sanitized hospital air. As I often remind people, it's not about me. My role here this day at Parkland Hospital is all about Katy. Supporting Katy through her ordeal and sharing news about Arielle isn't going to be accomplished if I don't get in there. My resolve set, one foot in front of the other, I finish the stretch of flooring and round the corner to Katy.

"Hi Katy. It's me, Michele."

I hunch over next to her so our faces are close. Her lips are so dry and damaged they are peeling in big chucks. They had removed her tube just two days prior and there is concern as to whether she will be able to speak after having been intubated for such a long period. Although Al spoke confidently of her speaking, watching her struggle to say every word is excruciating. She rolls her head from side to side, eyes darting wildly, forcing each word out slowly and painstakingly. Sometimes, in our impatience, we guess the word or phrase and sometimes we are right. She thanks me for taking care of her baby and I tear up. She brightens at the new photos and asks about Arielle. There is so little left of her, where her arms and legs once were there are simply heavily bandaged stumps. My brain is over loaded and my time is up. We will visit again tomorrow morning but for now Chris waits in the lobby for his turn.

I shed my blue ensemble and spell Chris from baby duty. Arielle sleeps in the stroller and I only have ten minutes before Al and Chris will be turned away due to the close of visiting hours. Ten minutes to reflect about that experience. I am shaking, tender, a little angry, a little scared, completely overwhelmed, emotional. Thank God she is alive and things seem to be improving. How is she going to function and who is going to take care of her? Who would take care of this baby? Being able to watch her three children grow and be there for them was gift enough. But my practical side was fraught with worry. I was glad to have come, grateful she was alive, happy to have seen her and emotionally fried to the max.

In Dallas. Your Dad hands you back over to me so he can see your Mom and handle the 7:00 a.m. doctor meeting. I go back and see your Mom at 11:00 a.m. Lunch at a great diner and then Chris, you and I hit the road home. You do fine until Huntsville. You start crying and keep it going for over four hours. Upon our return I give you a bath and a clean outfit. We sat outside and even went for a 30 minute walk. Noel dropped by in time for an evening bottle (one for each of us). I'm off to bed ~ exhausted.

Arielle, you and I are both playing catch-up from our weekend trip. Between the travel, the time change, the stress and the disruption of our schedules, we're pooped.

Kendrick spent his first day of Spring Break with us. The trip to the park was good use of a glorious day.

Your Mom has more GI bleeding and <u>another</u> emergency surgery.

Tonight you were less fussy and less spitty and spent most of the evening sleeping in my arms. Simply wonderful! Loved every minute.

Kendrick and Arielle

We are at the one month mark in Katy's medical journey. At some point early on, Al started blogging about Katy's condition at www.katyisstrong.wordpress.com linked through FaceBook. Thousands of us check in and see how Katy is doing. The medical jargon is mind numbing but Al does a great job of explaining things in simple terms. He writes well and infuses his intense love and dedication to his wife and her recovery in each entry.

But Al is a liar. He writes about her improvement in a way that makes her seem whole and she simply is not. And I don't mean whole in a sense of appendages, I mean more basic measures. For instance, Al will write that Katy is talking and asking for a hot dog. But when witnessing Katy communicating, it is a painful, time-consuming guessing game. When confronted, Al confesses to ensuring a sunny slant. Why? It seems that Al takes the time to read all the comments people are posting. One such response claimed that Katy's courage had given this unidentified man the willpower to continue living after thoughts of suicide. So many people were being touched by Katy's story, he wanted to give them hope too. Maybe Al is hoping himself or maybe he was too blinded by love to see what we saw. I don't fault him this discretion. I was lifted by his stories and closer to understanding my girlfriend's ordeal.

As the baby keeper, I am barraged with medical questions about Katy and her status. At times it truly is too much. Thankfully, I can direct scads of people to the blog and not have to flay open my friendship wounds, reliving her infections, surgeries too numerous to count, trials and setbacks. Like another helper on my team, the blog keeps us all connected. With no end in sight, we are all just hoping for continued improvement and a happy ending.

No naps today. You, Kendrick and I are busy this lovely spring day. You seem to be adjusting to your schedule, less colicky and eating better (more _in_ vs. _on_).

One last night at the rodeo to see Keith Urban. Aunt Betta takes you and we get to share secret giggles and baby talk about how wonderful you are.

Steve from Smoothie King called. They (Steve and his wife Marita) are good friends of your folks and remember seeing your Mom just before she had you. They are going to do a fundraiser, help us and say this is all they think about and they can't sleep.

Sleep Arielle. Enjoy the wonder of your new life and know that we are all here for you.

I brought you home last night and you slept in your carrier until 3:00 a.m. After a bottle, a burp, a diaper and a change in location, you went back to sleep until 7:00 a.m. Up we are to start our day and Kendrick (the four year old I nanny) is here too. I manage a lovely morning nap and feel well rested the whole day. Family time for you while Kendrick and I run a couple quick errands and I grab a workout at the gym. Karen and her son Logan come over for dinner and a slumber party. Girl talk and sharing have me up past 1:00 a.m. I'm really tired but want to share each day with you. Taking the time to journal these first days with you and chronicling your amazing life is one of the many ways I hope to make you feel cherished. :) Good night.

Arielle visits with Logan and Karen

Jo Daspit presents a donation to John Bohner, whose wife Jennifer has been spearheading fundraising efforts for the Hayes family.

Young mother of three continues fight for life

– Fundraisers scheduled to help family –

BY CHERYL "CJ" JOHNSON

The Tribune

Just weeks ago, Katy Hayes was a healthy, expectant mother who, after she delivered a healthy baby girl named Arielle, experienced complications. Hayes developed a Streptococcal A infection which shut down several organs, that eventually had to be removed. She was on dialysis and a ventilator; to save her life, due to the severe blood infection, the doctors said she would have to have all four of her limbs amputated.

On March 2, Hayes had surgery to remove both of her legs to just above her knees. Due to dead and infected tissue under her skin, the toxins were slowing her healing and it had to be removed. Two days later, Hayes had the surgery in which doctors amputated both of her arms to just above the elbows.

See HAYES/2D

HAYES

CONTINUED FROM 1A

There is good news on the horizon, however. Hayes had her breathing tube removed March 5 and her dialysis treatment was skipped to determine if she could function on her own.

During this enormously difficult and trying time, friends of Hayes and her husband ,Al, and much of the Kingwood community have rallied around the family. Help is coming from all directions and numerous fundraisers have also been planned. The couple are self-employed and they do not have the funds needed to cope with the mounting medical bills.

For those wishing to help Hayes and her family, visit *www.kingwoodmoyc.org*, or go to the Facebook group "Pray for Katy Hayes," send an e-mail to *KatyHayesFund@ yahoo.com*, or attend a fundraiser (see information box).

FUNDRAISERS FOR KATY HAYES AND FAMILY

You are really taking to your schedule. Up at 3:00 a.m. Ah! Your appetite is on the rise too.

You and I had lunch with Chef Karen at Pei Wei and watched you sleep and gesture with your hands. Errands and then home to fix dinner for Betta and Jake. Grilled salmon, grilled veggies, baguette, red wine and dark chocolate brownies with dried cherries. The evening was a bit cooler but we still went for a walk.

Bought you some toys and a pair of denim diaper covers. Also picked up some diaper changing items and netting for your stroller. Love you baby girl. I tell you 100 times a day and cover you with big, smacking kisses.

Texas-sized rose

Gorgeous day today! Aunt Betta came over and we took you for a nice, long walk through the neighborhood. You love being outside.

Nice volunteers (Susan and her grandson Dylan) gardened for me for a couple hours. Thank you!

I went out with Noel and Nelson tonight but I'm so exhausted I'm not much fun. Paula sits with you. Paula, myself and your Mom have all been MOYC president.

Please sleep better tonight. Tomorrow is your big TV interview with Channel 2. Don't worry, you'll be great! :)

Paula and Arielle

Profound and shocking events in our lives leave us with imbedded memories of the most mundane details. Like where you were when something catastrophic happened. The fact I was wearing my teal robe and fuzzy socks when I learned about Katy's hospitalization seems inconsequential. Although not on that magnitude, my own personal tsunami was arriving. My flannel, winter jammies are mismatched after Arielle spit up all over my first choice. Alas, this one doesn't make it very long either and I was soon sporting a t-shirt reserved for gym workouts. So as the doorbell rings Saturday morning, interrupting our lazy slumber, I throw on my robe, slip on some fuzzy socks and dash downstairs. Securing my barking beasts, I approach the door and through the glass I see the shape of a man. But I already know. Even knowing who, or what this man represents, it doesn't soften the blow of what was to come. My mind is racing and playing out the foreshadowing of today's caller. It had started so simply when my son returned from a Thursday night visit with his Dad.

"Mommy, Daddy got papers and I'm going to start living with him one week and you one week". He stated matter-of-factly.

"No no baby. Your Dad and I follow the standard possession order set out by a judge. We don't choose. And anyway, 50/50 is bad for kids and families and Texas just doesn't do that".

Two days later, my ex-husband sent me an email that he was suing me for custody of our child. A lot of emotions and questions rush at you when faced with such a conflict but the biggest for me was just confusion. Why would he try to take him away from me? What is he thinking? Will I lose my house? Even though it is the truth, it feels melodramatic.

Where would we go? Sam and the dogs and baby Arielle and myself take up a lot of space. Sam thrives under my care. He is happy, healthy, well-liked and doing well in school. I was not only a stay-at-home Mom but people paid me to help raise their children and now I have Arielle. My ex is well aware I have Katy's baby. What kind of monster accuses "the saint" of not being a good enough parent? For crying out loud, I think angrily, people are GIVING me their babies.

The man on my front porch has brought legal documents to serve me. Wow. I once loved the man I was married to and he claimed at one point to love me too. Here, three and a half years after our divorce, we've come to this.

"Are you Michele Dykstra?" he asks through the closed, leaded glass door.

I don't answer right away. I am very aware of my slumbered appearance, my fuzzy socks, flannel jammie bottoms, old t-shirt, teal robe, bed head and unbrushed teeth. For the next few seconds I can choose to be anyone I want to be. I can say no and he'll come back or I can say yes and get the ball rolling, take the next step in my own personal nightmare and proudly stand up. Luckily, I know myself really well and I love being me. Deep sigh, square my shoulders, stand up, open the door.

"Yes sir I am".

Angels must have been watching over me (I seem to have an unlimited supply of them) but this legal documents de-liveryman was a delight. He hands me the papers with a smile and a good luck and God Bless before walking back to his vehicle. I retreat back inside the safety of my own home shaking and with unsteady hands quickly locked the door behind me. Slightly sick to my stomach and full of adrenaline, something else was working in my head. I threw back the deadbolt, pull open the door and ran out into the cold morning to get that man's attention.

"Sir. I just wanted to say thank you. You were really nice about that and it made it a lot easier".

His gentle smile greeted me again as he shares that he feels it is the only way to handle it and again wishes me the very best. My mental headline reads "Single mother raising son and newborn while nannying and volunteering gets sued." What is this world coming too? Cocking my head to the side I listen up the stairs for sounds of a stirring baby. She has managed to sleep through all the noise, excitement and lawsuit introduction. I head for the shower, a new outfit and new outlook for a new day.

As lovely as it was yesterday, it is that miserable today. Cold, rainy and dark all day. Good weather for napping and reading.

The interview got pushed back, then cancelled. Nelson came over and changed my oil in the Jeep. Nelson, Alison and Stephanie joined us over RC's Pizza for lunch. Yum. Jim showed up and helped with housework, held you for an hour, fed you and changed you too.

Your Daddy came by. He needs to hurry back to Dallas but can't let go. He came down for Jake's birthday party but has been trying to arrange time for the two of you. He played the piano for you, held you, fed you, changed you, told you he loved you too.

Quick visit with dad

Good night's sleep and a wonderful morning nap (for both of us) got our Sunday started in a good direction. Steve and Marita came by with groceries and formula. They oohed and aahed over you. A quick car trip to The Woodlands had us house hunting. Back in time for HCLC Singles dinner ~ and a bottle for you. Family time with Amber, Jake, Betta and Grandma Lu gave me some alone time for Sam's return. He asked about you right away. You and I settled in to watch some TV. You puked down my left side, then my right side and of course, all over yourself. You are in your <u>third</u> outfit of the day ~ diva.

Love your smile! Love your dimples! Love the way you light up a room! Love all your pinkness! Love you! :)

Brown-eyed girls

W hat would I do without Britt? One of my dearest friends and my every morning phone call girlfriend, she's also the genius who set up the Care Calendar at the beginning of this journey based on our needs and requests and incorporated a system to organize help with meals, baby time and baby chores. Tuesdays is Suzanne and Lisa days. New friends to us and ones we can always count on to show up with wine and formula. These two angels have been placed in our path when we didn't even know how invaluable their smiles, warmth and friendship would be. Wednesday nights we have an unofficial visitor. Michelle comes over to visit and help with folding laundry or taking the recycling. But Michelle and Arielle's mother have something in common, huge boobs. Yes, I mean it, huge boobs. As a newborn, it is as though Arielle senses this commonality. Michelle will settle Arielle's head on her shoulder and drape her down her front, supporting her bottom, and sweet slumber comes quickly. My bony shoulder and small breast never seem to be quite as accommodating to her. This happenstance meant much quieter Wednesday nights and Michelle and I enjoy good quality time. Tracy stakes out Thursdays and is regular as clockwork. Since I have known Tracy for years, this became my day to run a quick errand and have my weekly lunch with Sam.

Others floated in and out with offers to do more. Melissa and Jennifer find time from their own kiddos to come help mine. Miss Zoe steps in as a surrogate mother to me and a ministry to Arielle. With her own grandchildren far away, her empty nursery provides a little baby sanctuary when I have a meeting with a lawyer across town. An accidental phone call had Amber (friend, not Katy's daughter) shipped over immediately to aid me. I hadn't known I needed aid until she shows up and proves so useful. Aid is good. Baby

Aid, I'm sure some famous rock band will put together a relief effort now. But alas, all our needs have been met, no, **exceeded** by the love and kindness of our caring Kingwood community.

Sleeps well on Michelle

Today marks your fifth week living here with us. We love having you here!

Holding you with my left and writing with my right. Your eyelashes and eyebrows grow thicker everyday. I keep hoping your lashes are as amazing as your brother Jake's.

You spit up an inordinate amount today. I even had to wash my <u>shoes</u> (and my purse, the floor, the chair, the wall and <u>you</u>.) Another three outfit day. My dear I wish I knew what to do to help you.

Let's sleep on it. Love you baby girl. You are crashed out on my shoulder. Off to bed for both of us.

Katy's situation is depressingly consuming. The longer she fights and carries on, the more we hope and plan and dream of a new life for her. A new life as a mother and wife with no arms and no legs. Daily conversations revolve around prosthetics and wheelchair options. Therapies, both mental and physical and concerns over whether Katy will be able to speak or how she'll go to the bathroom are daily topics. Transportation is an issue for this family of five and the type of wheelchair that Katy will need. There are deep concerns over their current two-story rental house which simply cannot accommodate the new Katy. Money is another touchy subject with Katy's income earning potential thwarted. The silver lining there is that the government wholeheartedly assures Al that Katy will be able to go back to work next year and continues to deny worker's compensation. Are you kidding? What about opportunities for Katy to participate in? What will she do now? And what about the trappings of her past life? A local mental health therapist tends to the family and steps in with answers to our queries. The question of what to do with all of Katy's work and personal belongings that she'll never use again is brought up. Everything is to be left as it is. Once Katy is home, assuming she comes home, things will be addressed in due time. Her bulky massage table, her nail polish, her shoes, her rings and bracelets all wait for her return.

A beautiful sunny day with you! I dressed you in lavender and off we went.

Spitty today but full of smiles. After school, Rachel, Clare and Jeannette brought Madeleine and Abby over to visit you. They made you a card and raised money for your care. They each took turns holding you and pronouncing you a beautiful baby.

Betta picked you up for family time and Sam and I went to a fundraiser for your family. Long talk with your Daddy tonight ~ he loves your Mama. Time to wake you up for your last bottle of the night.

P.S. Last two days you tinkled during your bath ~ silly girl.

Sometimes you sound like a kitten. Sometimes you sound like a piglet. Sometimes you sound like a bird. Sometimes you just sound like a baby.

Your hair naturally forms a mohawk. It is adorable. You have some distinctive cowlicks and a definite left part for styling. Your scalp is dry and we're trying to come up with some solutions.

People describe you as content, alert, strong, sweet, attentive and gorgeous.

Sam has been soothing you with songs. He is singing an Easter song this Sunday about waving palm branches. You love it!

We went to Mudpie Pottery and did a footprint craft of you sweetie...

Cuddles and cartoons

Tomorrow is your brother Jake's 6th birthday so we went and had lunch with him today. If your Mom was here, she would have taken you up to the school by now and showed you off. So we went and met his teacher and some other nice folks. Jake enjoyed his cheese pizza, apple slices, yogurt, apple juice and oatmeal raisin cookie.

You weigh 11 pounds 6 ounces. I took you to Merry-Go-Round to have you weighed and buy some denim shoes for you.

You are off your schedule today. Instead of big naps you are up and down and all over the place. Let's hope all this daytime activity helps you sleep well tonight.

I'm chanting, quietly, in my head, no one can hear me. It is an urgent message from me to Katy. It is a wish I wish most strongly. You see, Katy is not doing well, not doing well at all. She has had a 107° fever for several days now and her situation is as touch and go as ever. But today is her son Jake's birthday and she cannot die today. Yesterday, maybe tomorrow, but please Katy, please do not die today. Be strong and fight this but if you have to go, don't go today. Let your son turn seven in your absence but not with the news we all dread. Don't die today. Don't die today. Don't die today.

Aunt Betta is a rock star. She has given up her life in Colorado to live in your home and tend to your family's needs. And while she has no children of her own, she shines in her role of doting Aunt and has gone to great lengths to throw Jake a fun and happy birthday party. And success! The water balloons are a huge hit and the toys and the cupcakes. Years from now, Jake can recount how Aunt Betta dropped all his frosted cupcakes upside down on the way to the party. Luckily, they were in a lidded container and mostly salvageable and still delicious.

It was a wonderful party. It was a great day. And Katy lives.

What a big day we have planned. Cartoons in our jammies (you in my arms ~ Sam by my side) is a lovely way to start the weekend. Off to recycle. Then to the Bake Sale at On The Park. It seems I know quite a few people there (customers). Note: They raised $5500!

Lunch with your family and then we all head to the park for Jake's birthday. The boys enjoyed their spiky balls, water guns, cars, cupcakes and water balloons.

You stayed to play but Sam and I came home for some one on one time. Upon your return Sam went to sleep and we hung out on the back patio with Marta and Pete and a bottle of Bordeaux.

It was a lovely day. :)

Arielle and Aunt Betta at the park

Bake Sale for Katy! Sam's love of tractors makes me the proud owner of a cast iron, John Deere tractor-shaped cake pan. Since we want to help too, Sam and I make my famous green, John Deere tractor pound cake. We mix up a bunch of quality ingredients, infuse it with love, bake it to golden perfection and off to the Bake Sale to help support our friends. I'm willing to bet that another mother of a little boy who loves tractors will show up and not be able to resist that green confection.

PISTACHIO POUND CAKE

1 white cake mix
1 small package instant pistachio pudding
4 eggs
1 cup cold water
½ cup vegetable oil
A few drops of green food coloring too

Combine all the ingredients. Pour into a greased and floured John Deere tractor-shaped cake pan. Bake 50-60 minutes at 350°. Let cool before turning upside down and releasing. Enjoy!

We came home with a coconut pie that was out of this world delicious! Never before had I had such a wondrous pie. The filling was loaded with delicious, flaky coconut. Delicious!

How can we barely make it to church? It starts at 11:00 a.m. and we're racing to make it. Was suppose to attend 9:30 a.m. meeting but it certainly didn't happen. You did great at church and then fell asleep which allowed Sam and I to run two errands. Home for a bit before Betta fetches you for a visit. I get a 30 minute nap in the hammock. Sam is at a friend's for a few. Back home you insist on an early supper and doze off happily. I should be sleeping but am desperately trying to finish up some things. Cool nights and warm, sunny days make great sleeping weather. Sweet dreams...

Cool nights and warm days. When we go to bed it's a little warm upstairs but not quite time for A/C. So we sleep with a sheet. Then it starts getting cooler and I cover us all up. By morning, the 46° has created a chill in the air and we snuggle with hopes of sleeping in.

Arielle, you are a very strong baby. When I straighten your arms or legs for lotion you fight me. You are very expressive with your hands (splayed or touching) and your feet (one set of toes bent and the other wiggling). Your hair is a natural mohawk but even more so today. I think it is adorable. You are on my lap right now and SMILING. :)

In the middle of the night, Sam crawls in bed with me to snuggle. He then says, "Don't forget the 5 a.m. feeding." and falls fast asleep.

YOU SLEPT THROUGH THE NIGHT! HOORAY! :)
HAPPY HAPPY HAPPY! :)

Another first, you finally found your thumb. Welcome to the wonderful world of thumb sucking.

Back to that whole sleep thing, I blended your formula last night and it seems to agree with you. You fell asleep at 10:00 p.m. and woke up at 6:00 a.m. I got _six_ straights hours of sleep and have been doing the happy dance all day.

Another TV interview with you in the spotlight, helping your Mom. The story aired tonight and you were wonderful. It was you, Betta and me in the back yard doing a follow-up story with Channel 39 (Lettie). They did us right. :) Would really appreciate another good night's sleep sweetie pie.

Okay, Betta informs me that you sucked your thumb yesterday. She forgot to inform me. Regardless, we're all thrilled you are developing comforting methods. You are doing everything so well. <:) (that's your smile with a Mohawk)

Seven weeks old today! Ah! We had a lovely day and are enjoying our 80° spring weather.

You are getting so strong, I need both hands to hold you. You have been lifting and pushing up. Family time tonight was you, Jake and Aunt Betta. Jake fed you and rocked you while Aunt Betta "cooked".

Michelle came by for weekly baby time and chores. You puked so much she gave you another bath. Even she noted how much you loved your bath. Then she took you outside for some nice evening fresh air and she locked herself out.

The scratch on your face (from your fingernail) is still healing. Love you!

People say the strangest things to me. They call me a saint and an angel. I don't get it. As far as you are concerned, I was in the right place at the right time. You bring me a lot of joy. If only for a few stolen moments, I get to be a baby mama again. I truly feel that God has brought us together. I look forward to what he has planned for us. Let's enjoy the journey together!

Mother continues fight for life

By Cheryl "CJ" Johnson

The Tribune

Just six weeks ago, Katy Hayes, 41, was a healthy, happy, Kingwood mom who had just given birth to her third child, Arielle. But, within a week, things changed drastically. She went into a coma after contracting a mysterious infection which was later identified as Strep A. Although she delivered her baby at home with a midwife, family members have stated that the midwife "did everything right" and they have no idea how she contracted the infection.

Katy then had multiple organ failure which resulted in the removal of several organs, including the amputation of all four limbs.

The latest on her condition as of March 24 is that her husband arrived at a breathing mask which had previously been removed. Her condition had deteriorated overnight due to a collapsed lung which doctors believe was caused by pleural effusion. Cultures taken will determine what the actual cause of her breathing problem is.

"One possibility is simply that she is worn out. The doctor compared it to treading water for several days... eventually you would tire. Katy was resting well when I left her, but I hope that we are able to find more answers over the next day or two," said her husband, Al.

Due to the fact that Katy and Al are self-employed, there has been no paycheck coming in because Al has rarely left her bedside since their ordeal began. The community, including numerous strangers throughout the country, have fundraisers.

There will be a bake sale on March 27 from 10 a.m. - 4 p.m. at On the Park Toy Store in Kingwood, hosted by Rockin' On Moms of Kingwood/Atascocita.

On Sat., April 3 there will be a "Pink Parlor" at the Picnic in the Park at Town Center from 9 a.m. - 5 p.m. Bring the little princesses to get "glammed up" and there will be fun for the boys , too.

The Mom's Club International will hold a bake sale on April 10 from 11 a.m. to 1 p.m. in front of Kroger in Kingwood, at 3410 North Park Drive. Contact Dawn Engle at englemomma@yahoo.com or 352-999-2055 to donate baked goods which can be dropped off at her home the day before the event.

All proceeds with be donated to Katy and her family.

"Courtside for Kate" featuring Cliff players in the world, will be hosting a tennis clinic and luncheon at the Kingwood Country Club from 10 a.m. to 1:30 p.m., on Thursday, April 22.

Quest High School is sponsoring a garage sale to add their support to the Katy Hayes fund. It will be held on the grounds of Quest's former campus on Timber Forest Drive, on Saturday, April 24 from 8 a.m. to 4 p.m. Setup will begin at 6 a.m. For more information contact bellabeadshop@gmail.com, or call Karen at 281-812-3237.

Also on April 24 is the Hot -n-Classy Car Show sponsored by Chesmar Homes beginning at 10:30 a.m. at Hunter's Creek in Baytown.

On May 15, a second Hot-n-Classy Car Show will be held in Bay View - League City beginning at 10:30 a.m. For information on both events visit *www.*

Happy April Fool's Day!

A wonderful, sunny day. Melissa came over and helped with you. Karen brought Logan for lunch and play and we all spent lots of time outside. Betta and Pat picked you up for some family time. (Sam left tonight for a three day weekend).

Got some bad news today. Your Mama has pneumonia. I'm very concerned. We'll just have to hope for the best.

I'm exhausted after a long and active day. Trying to put the finishing touches on our day, like journaling. This journal made the news the other night. It's a bridge, for you Arielle.

6 a.m. and you're ready to start your day. We begin with some kangaroo love (skin on skin) and you promptly threw up all over me. You had a nice nap just in time for me to welcome Barry and Gill. They (Allison's folks) drove in from Houston to garden for us. They also brought you a gift card and a gift for Sam. I helped until it was time to tend to you and then go to The Gathering Place. Gill was thrilled to get some time with you.

At family's house last night they told tales of a monstrous poo that no diaper could contain. You do everything so well!

You have a rash on your chest and neck. I'm not too worried but I am going to keep an eye on it.

Today is Picnic in the Park at Town Center. The Pink Parlor booth will turn you into a princess or a pirate and all proceeds help your family. We will definitely make an appearance.

Oh, we're exhausted. You are eating exceptionally well (and a lot) so we think a growth spurt is in order. The event today was a tremendous success. Very well attended, a fabulous location and fun. We got a little toasty but came home to cool down. You visited your family for a few hours and now, here. Sucking your left thumb and rubbing the back of your head with your right hand. Betta leaves tomorrow for a couple weeks ~ she will miss you.

Betta says you rolled over. A major milestone and time to start strapping you into things.

Photo by JENNIFER SUMMER/The
Observer

New Caney resident Amy Yeoman
gets glammed up at the Pink Parlor
booth where proceeds benefited
Katy Hayes at the annual Picnic on
the Park celebration April 3.

HAPPY EASTER! And happy mommy and happy baby. You slept completely through the night again! Oh joy! From 10 p.m. to 7 a.m. And I slept almost the same amount of time. With so little sleep, I struggle to stay healthy. Yesterday, I wasn't feeling my best. Today, much better. Thank you.

What an active day we've had. You've hardly slept at all which I hope translates into a good night's rest. You are a happy and easy baby. Amrita came by today for around an hour and we had some quality time. Easter dinner at Stephanie's with her family. Sam returns and dotes on you. You are cluster feeding constantly. You're falling asleep with a thumb in your mouth and one rubbing your head. I'm really proud of you! :)

MILESTONES: purposeful grabbing and recognizing people. My darling you have changed <u>so</u> much in such a short time. Your quirks and personality are beginning to become more apparent. You wake up happy and rested and don't scream, just coo. You still love your bath and have gotten better about me pulling clothes over your head. You are also less messy when eating. Still a puker — but less mess when eating. You can sleep through anything or not sleep at all. You are definitely going through a growth spurt. It seems I can't feed you enough. You hold my finger that holds the bottle. You suck your left thumb. You've started holding onto the blanket or your outfit. You are good with all people. You are a wonderful, healthy, pink miracle.

Two ladies, Christian and Stephanie, came over and loved on you <u>and</u> cleaned the house top to bottom. It wasn't that dirty to begin with but it's <u>all</u> clean right now. Sent the dogs to the groomers (gee it's quiet) and we're all just enjoying you.

Busy day and you hang out with me at night. I hope you sleep well my dear.

TWO MONTHS OLD! Tada! My darling you are such a treasure. And how you have grown. Since we spend every day together, sometimes the changes creep up on me. You could not be more beautiful, you are communicating your likes and needs, you are getting stronger too. Your schedule is in a constant state of flux. However, you slept through the night last night. This is a trend we should embrace. To accomplish this you are ravenous every two hours and hardly nap. Your smile lights up the room and you coo and gurgle to everyone's delight. Keep being you sister! You do it <u>all</u> so well.

Tough day for your Dad which means a tough day for your Mama. Tough day for Grandma Pat too. Two lovely strangers, Suzanne and Lisa, came and helped and shopped for us today. Never forget how amazing this community has been ~ supporting us during this difficult time.

Good morning. I'd like to start the day by thanking you for sleeping. :)

A very productive day for me. For you, lots of rest. No family visit today but plenty of quality time with people who love you (like me).

Tonight, when I was feeding you, you placed a hand on either side of the bottle and held it. It only lasted a minute but it is another milestone. Aunt Betta called from Colorado to check on you but we were out. Between you and me, you're doing just fine...:)

There are a lot of questions that people ask daily. I have never addressed these questions here until now. How long will the baby live with me? What will you do when she goes home? So let's talk about it. As long as you need a place to live Arielle, you are welcome here. When you do leave to go home, my heart will break. I hope we find a way to maintain a relationship. I love you. I love you and care for you and mother you. We do all the things I did with my own baby. We go on walks, do footprint art, I take your picture constantly, I video you, I sing to you, I take you to church. You are part of our family and firmly placed in my heart.

Snuggling on a cold day

Off to Sam's drizzly soccer game. We were supposed to go downtown to the Children's Festival but cancelled due to the weather. Logan and Karen stayed for a play date and some pink time (respectively). Dashed over to Smoothie King for a Katy Hayes Fundraiser and introduced them to smoothies. Yum! Stephanie dropped by and waltzed with you while I put Sam to bed.

Your smile lights up your entire face and any room you are in. No family time this weekend because they are in Dallas to see your Mom and Dad. I'm enjoying our time together.

Can I take a moment to let you know how much I appreciate you sleeping so much at night? Thank you.

A busy day but you slept well during the day. We stopped by the family's house for 15 minutes between things. Grandma Pat and Daddy Bill returned from Dallas and return to Michigan tomorrow. I wanted them to be able to say good-bye. Lucille and Jake got a minute with you too.

Miss Zoe from KUMC came over and just held you. For three hours you either slept snuggled up against her, ate, or lay on your back cooing and smiling. You are such a delightful child!

You have really taken to sucking your thumb. We started our day early and Sam joined us in the nursery. I commented on your thumb sucking. Sam beams at me and confesses "I snuck in here at night and taught her that".

You slept well today and haven't been as ravenous. We walked Sam to school and you fell asleep. I strolled you right into the kitchen and let you snooze.

Grandma Lu came over to visit you tonight. We went on a nice walk. Trying to get you to bed earlier as we evolve into yet another schedule. Now I'm running around (late) prepping bottles, prepping lunches, doing laundry, answering emails.

After a good night's sleep you wake up delighted and delightful. Grinning and cooing you poke your tongue out. You're learning more about your tongue and like to stretch and wiggle it. Very cute.

Since you spit up so much, there is <u>tons</u> of laundry. From outfits, burp cloths, bibs, washcloths, changing pad covers and <u>me</u>, all of my clothes. This morning I changed your poopy diaper, took off your outfit and gave you your morning bath. Then I grabbed up all that laundry to throw in the wash. Just in time I realized I had grabbed the dirty diaper too. That would have been super gross.

I'm going to try and sneak a nap...

How has <u>my</u> life changed?

I used to go to the gym regularly ~ maybe three times a week. Now I average once a month. I used to pursue dating and jobs. I used to spend my off-weekends indulging myself and going out with friends. I used to bathe regularly and dress-up without fear of vomit. I have accepted you fully into my life and understand that part of our union, is the release of <u>my</u> reality into <u>our</u> new life. Strangers do for us what I once did daily. I skipped haircuts for two months. I plan my vacations with you in mind. Everything has changed.

The family claimed you already had a baby book. I asked for it. I felt it might be time to either begin it or at least document your development. What a beautiful surprise...your Mom had already filled it out. In her own handwriting, in her own words, she described herself, her life, her feelings for you and her hopes for her family's future. What a gift ~ a treasure. I was so happy for you. I am so proud of Katy and am heart-wrenchingly grateful on your behalf. I got goose bumps just reading her words. Never doubt how much your Mama loved you from the very beginning.

Wine night with Paula and Erin.

This special story of baby's beginning
belongs to

Arielle Elisabetta Hayes

Foot Prints

Getting Prepared

Mother's preparations I had 2 showers at our house. I was busy working - exercizing and preparing clients for my baby down-time. Also getting my mothers group ready for me being gone.

Father's preparations

Preparations at home We had to clean out Daddies office upstairs to make it your room. We set up Jakes trundle bed for guests. We want to paint it green + purple.

Still sleeping through the night and I love you for it. Up at 5 a.m. and then back down (after a feeding) until 7:15 when we normally start our day. Lunch with Sam and a great afternoon nap. Visit the family and then Britt took over so I could have some adult time. Dinner and drinks with Stephanie and Denise. Much fun. I come home to you and melt. Ready myself for bed and lie on the floor, staring at you, listening to you breathe. I love you very much. Your eyelashes amaze me. You are a wonderful baby. Sleep well my dear as we embrace tomorrow. Remember Arielle, every day is a gift. That is why it is called the "present". :)

Quality time with Britt

Sometimes, journaling can be a real challenge. During our time together I'll think about what I want to share with you about our day. My intent is to share with you a great sense of love and belonging. You are the most delightful baby. You are sweet and beautiful. You are a good eater and a better burper. You are easy-going and good-natured. You self-soothe and sleep through the night. You are a bit of a celebrity and everybody wants to spend time with you. Each day is new and exciting as you grow and evolve. You are good-sized and your 3-6 months clothes will be too small soon. You are using your hands more and like to hold your outfit. You do everything so well.

Your family made me a little crazy today. I get very protective and therefore frustrated when they seem unable to care for you for a few hours. They should know the basics. Deep breath. We're all fighting some kind of battle. They do love you so.

Dear Michele,

Thank you so very much for volunteering to care for Arielle during this very difficult time for our family. Your generosity has overwhelmed us. Arielle is obviously thriving under your excellent care and we know that you will continue to be a large part of her life well after she returns home to her family. You will always have a very special place in all of our hearts.

Since you have refused to receive payment for your services, we sincerely hope that you will accept the enclosed funds to help off-set any expenses you are incurring related to Arielle's care that are not covered by the donations you have received on her behalf.

We recognize that caring for a newborn requires a tremendous amount of sacrifice and energy which money cannot replace, but we hope that perhaps you can use a portion of these funds to make life a little bit easier for your family - consider a massage, a day at the spa, a house cleaning service, or a fun outing with Sam.

We are forever grateful to you,

The Hayes Family

Church this morning and visitors the rest of the day. You got overtired and I'm exhausted. You get lots of visitors and since they are here for <u>you</u>, I don't feel I can say no (often). But I also feel I need to play hostess and naps and cleaning suffer mightily.

You know me. Here are some things you might not know. I grew up in Michigan, like your Mom. Your Mom and I also share a birthday by ten days (she's older). I'm passionate about life and choose to be happy, surround myself with things I love and live abundantly. Our two black labs welcome you here and Sam dotes on you. Managed to plant a vegetable garden in patio pots and love our Spring breezes in the evening. Life is a great journey and I'm thrilled we're sharing a path.

I call myself "Mama" to you. At first I was ashamed. But my dear, I want you to get a true mothering and the benefits a mother's love offers. Even if only for a brief time, I will gladly be your Mama and love you as my own.

Coo. Babble. Roar. Coo. You make amazing sounds. Strong and alert you grow bigger and stronger every day. You sleep in a leopard-print, slanted pillow that I call your recliner. You love it. You hold my fingers or the bottle every time. I've started using bibs on you more and it's helped. Cool and rainy today ~ surprising for April. Betta and Tom have returned and your after school visits will resume.

Pet names I have for you: Pink, The Pink Princess, Peanut, Sister, Darling, Happy, Spitty-Up Girl

You are the most wonderful baby in the whole wide world. You slept for <u>12</u> hours last night. Don't think all my praise and adoration is a direct result of your sleeping abilities. You have a sweet disposition and are simply an easy baby.

Tonight Betta tells me about a plan to have you start spending one night a week at your home. Then they want to increase that to two nights a week and more until you are home full time. I can't quite imagine this. They are your people and I know you need to go. I will miss you so.

Saw the therapist earlier today to discuss our situation and the eventual separation. What apropos timing.

Today was a busy, yet productive day. I've had more time to consider the family's wishes/plans to start keeping you overnight. I want to be supportive of this but...you're MY baby now and I'll miss you and I don't want to let you go. Something for me to work on. Heather came to sit with you while I had lunch with Sam and picked up photos of you for the album. Then you napped and then over to the family's. I missed you today. I look forward to seeing your grin when you wake up and covering you with kisses.

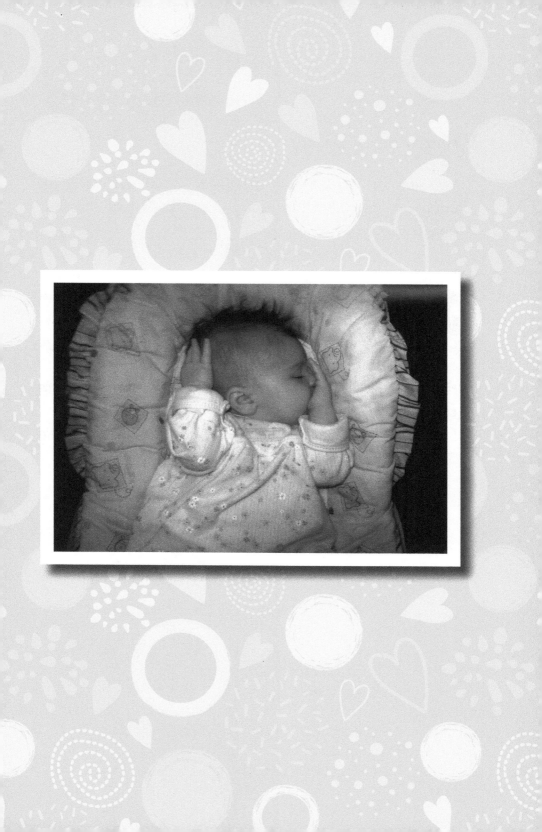

Happy Earth Day!

You slept for <u>12</u> hours straight! What an amazing baby you are. :) When you wake up so well-rested, you smile and coo all day.

Courtside for Katy Tennis Clinic fundraiser earned $12,500. today. We were invited for lunch and showed up to smile and greet the community. Channel 11 interviewed us. Strange news coverage about home birth vs. hospital birth. Whatever. Still prepping your stuff (and your handlers) for your big trip to Dallas this weekend. I'm going to miss you. I'm searching for the positive in all this and am sure Sam will benefit from my undivided attention.

Courtside for Katy, other fundraisers raise funds for Hayes family

By JENNIFER SUMMER
jsummer@hcnonline.com

While standing in line to purchase food at the Katy Hayes fundraiser at Skeeter's Mesquite Grill March 4, Tanya Robinson struck up a conversation with others in line to pass the time.

"I talked to a man who was in line behind me and it turned out to be Katy's dad. I do not know Katy personally but speaking with her father made me emotionally invested in her family and her story. I knew there was something more I could do," Robinson said.

Robinson, an avid tennis player, spoke with the director of tennis for the Kingwood Country Club, Randy Mattingley, about a possible fundraiser. They developed the idea of a special fundraiser for the community, Courtside for Katy, to be held April 22 at 10 a.m.

The event will co-mingle

Submitted photo

The Kingwood Country Club tennis group, made up of Keith Dollar, Matt Stolt, Randy Mattingley, Kirk Keller, Teddy DeBlasi, Jason Reid, pictured, and Lee Wright and Johnna Thomson, not pictured, is looking forward to helping with the Courtside for Katy Hayes Tennis Clinic and Luncheon which will serve as a fundraiser for the Hayes family.

Submitted photo

The Kingwood Country Club tennis team made up of Jill Wolocko, Anita Flematti, Jill Jones, Kelly Ferguson, Jill Weller, Christy Duncan, Tanya Robinson, Alice Jones, Mary Vosloh, Jill Curtis and Nancy Rivier-Rogers is looking forward to helping and hosting guests at the Courtside for Katy Hayes fundraiser April 22.

Robinson said.

"I also spoke with Paula Tobey who has organized and helped with the fundraisers around the community and is a close friend of Katy's, she said Katy was very excited because she was very active herself."

Katy Hayes is a Kingwood

hope she has a peaceful night's sleep."

There are additional fundraisers for the Katy Hayes fund such as the following:

■ Mom's Club International Bake Sale at the Kingwood Kroger on Northpark Drive, April 10

"Randy had spoken with the Richeys about a possible fundraiser for the Mental Health Association but was trying to find a way to tie it to the community. With my idea for the fundraiser for Katy, the two worked perfectly together," Robinson added.

Around 80 percent of the funds raised will benefit Katy Hayes and her family, and approximately 20-percent of the proceeds will benefit the Mental Health Association.

Cliff Richey will speak at the luncheon about his bouts with depression and how he overcame the disease, which is the topic of his book. Every guest who signs up for the tennis clinic and/or the luncheon will receive an autographed copy of Cliff's book and a T-shirt.

"The Richeys are very excited to be a part of this fundraiser, and to combine the two fundraisers is amazing,"

tiple organ failure and in the course of treatment, her limbs had to be amputated.

She has been responsive but is still fighting for life. Before falling ill, Katy was the president of Mothers Against Young Children, so that group as well as many people from the community have stepped forward to help raise funds for the Hayes family.

In an update from Katy's husband, Al's, blog, he writes, "Katy has been battling a high fever all day. I came in to her being at 105.9, and left her at 105.1. They did a CT scan of her chest and abdomen. The results won't be in until later, and the final read won't be available until tomorrow morning. The scans were to see if there is any infection causing the fever. There is a possibility that the spleen is infected where it is damaged. More of the "wait and see" game. I just

by Chesmar Homes in Baytown, April 24

■ Community garage sale at the former Quest High School Campus, April 24

Courtside for Katy is available for Kingwood Country Club members and non-members. There will also be a silent auction and raffle at this particular fundraiser.

"This fundraiser is great because it is something everyone can be a part of because the clinic will benefit any range of tennis player from beginner to the professional level," Robinson said.

For more information about Courtside for Katy, e-mail Tanya Robinson at tanyabeth@earthlink.net.

For more information about Katy Hayes, donations, fundraisers or how to help, log on to www.facebook.com/group.php?gid=343063085090.

Tennis clinic and luncheon benefiting Katy Hayes raises $12,500

More than 70 people participated in the tennis clinic fundraiser, "Courtside for Katy," held at Kingwood Country Club April 22.

BY CHERYL "CJ" JOHNSON
The Tribune

Another fundraiser benefiting the Katy Hayes fund has turned out to be a smashing success. A tennis clinic held by local pros Joe Snailum, Jay Berry and Fernando Mateu, along with staff pros Lee Wright, Keith Dollar, Jason Reid, Kirk Keller, Teddy diBlasi, Matt Stolt and Johnna Thompson from Kingwood Country Club, boasted more than 70 participants Thursday.

After the tennis clinic, more than 100 people were signed up for the luncheon and silent auction held in the clubhouse at the Kingwood Country Club. Former top 10, world-ranked tennis players Cliff and Nancy Richey were featured guests at the event, and Cliff Richey gave the keynote speech.

Cliff also authored a book, "Acing Depression-A Tennis Champion's Toughest Match," which chronicles his life-long battle with clinical depression. Originally, he was in town to promote his book and give

Coordinators of the event Randy Mattingley, tennis director for the Kingwood Country Club; Tanya Robinson, friend of the Hayes;' Michele Dykstra, also a friend of the Hayes', holding baby Arielle whom she has been caring for since Katy's hospitalization; and Mike Feilds, the GM for the Kingwood Country Club.

proceeds from it to the Mental Health Association, but when he heard about Katy Hayes' plight, he decided to give all proceeds from his book to her fund. Richey autographed copies of his book for participants after the luncheon.

"Adversity causes some to break, and others to break records," said Randy Mattingly, the tennis director for the Kingwood Country Club who was instrumental in helping to put the event together, along with Tanya Robinson, a good friend of the Hayes family.

Katy Hayes is a young local mother who, a week after giving birth to daughter Arielle, contracted a deadly Strep A infection which has resulted in over two months of hospitalization, the loss of all four limbs which were removed due to dead and infected tissue, and the removal of several of her organs, among other issues. Katy and her husband, Al, are self-employed and have no medical insurance; so there have been many fundraisers to help the family with their mounting medical costs.

People. There are people who know your Mom and/ or your Dad. There are people who know your story. This "situation" has introduced me to a group of people I could never have imagined. Strangers who give, strangers who donate, strangers who cry, strangers who care. Some of them track me down to chat. Others share their stories. Others just want information or the chance to share in the joy, which is you. Stopped by Designer Consignor and saw Tina. Boy did she embrace you! She also shared that she raised a relative's baby for one year and how she loved Lily like her own and how crushing it was to give her back to her family. I appreciated her openness. Few understand the depth of my love for you and the bond we have created.

I DVRed Private Practice, only to be faced with a similar story. Violet returns and wants to be Lucas' Mom. Addison (dating "father" Pete) has been filling the traditional mother role and is devastated at the thought of losing this child, and this child's love, to the biological mother. Hmmm.

Moved the futon out of the office. Put the glider in there with a side table and a donated Peter Rabbit lamp. It truly looks and feels like a real nursery now. Perhaps I'll accept the offer of a crib now.

Your big trip to Dallas to see your Mom. Betta, Tom, Jake and Lucille will be here early for your second trip to Dallas and your first trip away from me. I'm a little nervous. I am going to miss you. Up late last night packing all your little (but many) pink accoutrement. I am sure you will spark joy and hope in your mother's heart.

Sam and I have soccer and an Art Fair for kids. Then Allison from Austin visits, a party with Renee and Kris, home for Allison's birthday cake and champagne. Looking forward to bike rides and reading with my son.

Hurry home!

My alone time with Sam is a gift ~ but we all await your return. When Tom pulls into the driveway, we rush out to greet you with smiles. Ah! Sweet girl! Betta and Tom have cared for you well. You have a tiny diaper rash but that's expected for the seven hours of roundabout driving you did. I give you a quick bath and a clean outfit. Off to bed Arielle. Welcome home.

A fussy night but all in all not so bad. Working our way back into a bit of a routine. It's a delight to have you back. I must confess, the time apart was healthy. It gave me a bit of perspective about our relationship. It allowed me to miss you and revel in your homecoming. You were such an angel for Tom and Betta, I half expected them to just keep you. I'm not ready.

Bath time

A kind and generous compliment from your Daddy has me smiling. First off, your Mom is a rock star! Perhaps your visit was the push she needed. Her recovery in the last week has surpassed all expectations. The plan, to move her out of ICU tomorrow. What joy! I get teary and grin with hope and possibility. Your Dad was explaining the next step and the return to Kingwood. Yes, Kingwood. Up 'til now there had only been talk of transfer to a Houston-based rehabilitation center. Home. They are bringing her home. I miss her and can't wait to talk to her. Can't wait to tell her a blunt joke and make her laugh. Selfishly, I inquired as to how this impacts our current situation.

In my arms, you hold my necklace as you rest your head on my chest. You feel so right in my arms. With your Mom returning, I hope she can accept my arms around you.

Another rough night. Your third night home from Dallas and your schedule is still completely off. I'm getting around five hours of sleep a night. I really need a nap. Mary Kay (Shears 'n Action) did my highlights today and I fell asleep. Suzanne and Lisa came over and bathed you, organized donations and brought gifts. Thank you!

You look so peaceful, cherubic, when you sleep. Betta dropped you off tonight and stayed for a glass of wine. We talked about life, your Daddy, what the future may hold and spent time getting to know each other. She is going to start picking you up in the afternoons after she picks up Jake. She and I can visit until you wake up. Off to bed.

Announced your progress at church tonight to a round of applause. Everyone is happy to hear good news about your Mama.

Children's Assistance Foundation fundraiser to benefit Hayes family

By JENNIFER SUMMER
jsummer@hcnonline.com

Since 1999, the Children's Assistance Foundation, started by the owners of QLS Family Fitness Kyle and Monica Bauer, has helped raise funds for residents affected by illness or an accident.

When the Bauers began to plan this year's fundraiser, Katy Hayes and family came to mind, so they sat down with her friends and asked how they could help.

"We met with the Bauers where they could ask us if we just wanted them to donate money or to organize an event for the community where they could raise money for Katy and her family," Jennifer Bohner, close friend of Katy's, said. "We decided on the event because it will be something everyone can enjoy and it will be a lot of fun."

QLS will host "A Night Under the Stars" fundraising event May 1 for the whole family. The fundraiser will include several different events such as a children's fashion show, tasting of foods from local restaurants, bingo, dessert, an adult fashion show and live auction, and a middle school dance.

All of the proceeds raised from this event will benefit Katy, who is fighting a Strep A infection that developed in her uterus shortly after giving birth to her third child, Arielle.

Because of the infection, Katy has undergone numerous life-

See HAYES, Page 9A

HAYES
Continued from Page 8A

saving surgeries where several of her organs have been removed and all limbs amputated above the middle joint.

"We are very excited about this event because we have already received a great response from the community and QLS has been so helpful. They do a great job throwing these fundraisers," Bohner said.

The children's fashion show still has a couple of spots left where the models can wear their favorite outfit or a costume and strut for the audience. The fashion show participants receive a trophy and a professional photograph as keepsakes.

The "Taste of the Town" features food donated by local restaurants - Cedar Landing Marina, Wazabi, Roma's New York Pizzeria and Schlotzky's. Lawler's Cheesecake will provide the desserts for the dessert portion of the night, and the Atasca Oaks Starbucks donated the coffee.

The organizers have collected great prizes such as laptops for bingo winners, and silent and live auction items like sporting event tickets, trips and a day on the set of "Friday Night Lights" in Austin for guests to bid on.

"This is a full family event with a lot of activities throughout the night we hope will raise money for Katy. The fundraiser is also a good chance to teach kids the importance of helping others in need and fundraisers," Bohner added.

The middle school dance has some room for those of age. All of the tables are sold but individual tickets are still available for the community.

In addition to "A Night Under the Stars," there has been a variety of there other fundraisers in the community to help raise funds for Katy and her family.

"The way the community has stepped forward to help Katy is amazing. Students of Al's, Katy's husband, in the River Oaks area hosted a concert that raised almost $8,000, and others who knew Katy have organized their own fundraisers to help them," Bohner said.

One of their largest fundraisers will be titled "A Night at the Museum" at the Houston Museum of Natural Science July 10.

Organizers are still in the beginning phases of securing bands and entertainment, but Brett Cullen is set to be one of the emcees.

"We invited everyone to join us for all of the fundraisers they can because they are fun for the whole family and it is for a good cause, to help Katy," Bohner added.

A NIGHT UNDER THE STARS

- **WHEN:** May 1, 5-10:30 p.m.
- **WHERE:** QLS Family Fitness, 20515 West Lake Houston Parkway, Atascocita
- **INFO:** 281-812-6963; jenniferb@scterm.com; http://katyhayesfund.giving.officelive.com

Another neck sighting. You are getting so strong. You love to look around and take it all in. Your neck has finally appeared! Just a crease is there but it's a neck! (Usually holding some milk drops hostage.)

We've changed your family routine ever so slightly. Now Betta swings by with Jake after she picks him up. They show up around 2:15 p.m. It's nice for me to have a little more time, time alone and the chance to walk or bike the kids home.

The last couple of nights have you down at 8 p.m., up at 3:30 a.m. for 45 minutes and starting your day around 7:00 a.m. Now if only I could get to bed at a reasonable time.

Trimmed your nails this morning. They grow so quickly and sharp. Trying to keep face scratches to a minimum.

It's an overcast and rainy end to our week. I love it. Usually I'd bake but we had big plans today. We went to church to set up for the Media Sale. Then, since this is his weekend away, we had lunch with Sam. Pei Wei. Home for your lunch and naps. While you're gone I worked diligently on the nursery. Restocking, sanitizing, arranging, decorating. I hope your room shows you the loving commitment we have taken to make you feel welcome. I'm waiting for your return. Would you like to take a quick stroll around the block?

Our evening walk ~ the best part of our day. You <u>love</u> nature. Talked to your mom tonight. Boy, I've really missed her. She sounded exhausted and I couldn't hear her over your ruckus. It was a busy morning, recycling and soccer. Too much time in the muggy weather and in the bucket (car seat). Betta came over so I could run to the grocery store. Michelle came over a little later, mostly because she missed you. It gave me a chance to get ready for the big QLS fundraiser. Quite an event! You were a stunner. Home for a stroll. Managed to get you to bed on time and settled in to watch Avatar. I found it depressing or maybe I'm just feeling a little lonely. It was a good day. I just need a good night's sleep. Off to bed...11:40 p.m.

Arielle's fundraiser outfit: The color theme was black and white, casual. Not the easiest "baby girl" colors. Luckily, I found an old, too big, Christmas dress someone had donated. It was black and white checked outfit. It had a broad, black, velveteen collar with lace trim and red roses. I cut the collar off with a pair of scissors. Then, I cut the legs off to make it a dress. A white diaper cover, white and black socks (that look like you're wearing Mary Janes) and a big, pale pink head bow/flower. Too cute!

You slept through the night again. 11 straight hours. You are so happy this morning and drained 7 1/2 ounces. Now we're planning out our day. Lovely.

Spent a few hours at church today. The ladies in the nursery really enjoy holding you.

You know I never journaled for Sam (my son) like this. Oh sure, I documented cute things, all the firsts and the like but not like this. I want your Mama to be able to "experience" your beginning. I see your Mom and I sitting down and us laughing and sharing all these details about you Arielle, and your first few months of life.

A secret supporter left beautiful purple tulips and a note on the front porch for me. The note reads, "Michele, Thanks for all you do. Have an awesome day. God bless. :)"

Betta ran late returning you tonight. You were so fussy this evening Betta couldn't get dinner ready (fajitas). Seems you were fairly inconsolable for around an hour. You seem overly tired to me. Strange since you slept all night last night and napped well today. I will put you straight to bed and will follow soon.

I'm at a bit of a crossroads. The lovely little, spiral-bound journal I fill in each night is alas, full. Against all odds, Katy is expected to make a full recovery. We are so grateful that she will be with us again. But looking down at the lavender hydrangea and butterfly print on the cover of the journal, it seems a little silly. Babies can't read and she's so busy growing this may seem insignificant. Katy won't be well enough to chat about the past any time soon. Why did I write these? Why do I force myself to find the time night after exhausted night to write this story? I'm having this conversation with myself because I can't decide if I should stop or if I should buy another journal and continue Arielle's documentation of life and love. Journaling is supposed to be good for your mental health and it's a very affordable past time. I wonder briefly if this diary has been more for me, but no, it truly has been a gift for them. Decision made, a trip to Gayle's Hallmark garners another lined journal and another day of adventures with Katy's baby.

A new day, a new journal. A normal day of being delighted by your smiles, sweet nature and good naps. I got to talk to your Mom this morning. We got off the phone and I called her right back. I felt like what I had said might have been the "wrong" thing to say ~ insensitive. She seemed confused. I want to say the right thing to help her. Jake finally lost his tooth today. Heard some upsetting news from my lawyer today. I know this has nothing to do with you, but it greatly impacts me. Hoping the morning meeting with the lawyer will answer some questions.

I look forward to tomorrow and spending it with you.

Happy 3 months old!

To celebrate turning three months old, you got up at 4:00 a.m., drank a big bottle, puked all over my jammies and were up for almost an hour. You had a wonderful, happy day. You eat around every two hours during the day.

Jennifer came by and took a bunch of pictures of your grin and dimples. You really put on a show.

Went to the last night of WOW (church) and everybody wanted to peek at you and ask about your Mama. Sleep well my friend.

Arielle visits with Pastor Barb

This morning you held your own breakfast bottle. What a big girl. Now it's time to make some changes. You're ready for a different nipple size on your bottle, rice formula and a crib.

Busy, busy day getting ready for Sam's birthday tomorrow. Moved the buffet out of the "nursery" and plan on setting up a crib or the pack-n-play. Betta has started talking to me about plans to bring your Mom home. I'm excited to see her. These plans also include you seeing your Mom daily and moving home. It's a lot to take in. We'll keep talking and planning and embracing change. I can't imagine you not being here, but we knew this day would come.

Grandma had special baby time with you this morning. After my quick errand, I hurried home to see you before your first nap. You were fed, burped, bathed and changed. I took you in my arms and SPLAT! You puked all over the kitchen floor and yourself and soaked my shoulder. You helped us celebrate Sam turning seven by joining us for lunch. At The Gathering Place, you smiled and charmed during my five minute yoga class.

Moved the buffet out of the office and tonight, for the very first time, you are sleeping in the pack-n-play.

Big talks with your Dad tonight. You'll be just fine ~ everybody loves you so.

HAPPY BIRTHDAY SAM!

Note: Top secret reveal from your Daddy about your Mom.

The doctors have said that Katy will probably be hospitalized and recovering for two years. Obviously, they underestimated Katy and how determined she can be. Now there is talk of sending her not to another hospital but to her own bed in her own home surrounded by her own friends and own family. It's stunningly happy news and we are eager for more good news. Details aren't forthcoming and hospital bureaucracy seems to rear its ugly head when least welcome. This is all very hush-hush but all in the inner circle know and our anticipation is barely containable.

One of Katy's supporters has a plan to welcome Katy home in style. Mary Kay wonders if it would be alright with the family to organize a welcome home line of people on the main road to the Hayes home with signs, smiles and waving well-wishers. My mind reels at the logistics it would take to coordinate the four plus hour drive from Dallas with a prone quadriplegic who hasn't left the hospital in months. She can't sit up for any amount of time. The message is loving but is it a bit too much? I bring it up with Al who is genuinely touched by such thoughtfulness. With plans to discuss again at a later date, the plan is put on hold. It's still really nice to have a plan, a plan where Katy comes home.

You fit so neatly in our lives, you're just one of the gang. Grandma and Grampy are here. We all loaded up (you, Sam and me and G &G G) and went to watch an early morning soccer game. Quick stop at Lowe's and lunch at Bill's Cafe. Cindy came and watched you during Sam's bowling birthday party. Your family is back in Dallas this Mother's Day weekend to see your Mom. I'm so tired I'm getting a headache. This is such a busy weekend.

Cindy smiles

Front page news and it's a love story. Pictures and words depicting your Mom's ordeal, her battle and your Dad's steadfastness. I truly believe your Dad saved your Mom's life. Both your folks have been awe-inspiring.

I told Sam "thank you for making me a Mom" and I told you the same thing too. Even if we're just playing house, I have all the mother responsibilities, worries, joy and hope. Our time together is a gift I treasure.

Recently, I was writing about our situation and made a typo. While typing mother, I skipped the "m" and it read "I feel like her other". Perhaps it is the most poetic error of truth. I am your other.

HOUSTON ★ CHRONICLE

★chron.com
THE GOOD LIFE

SUNDAY, MAY 9, 2010   ★ ★ ★   VOL. 109 · NO. 208 · $2.0

ROBIN HOOD IN LEGEND

Travel to St. Mary's Church in Nottingham in search of the real Robin Hood. **PAGE J1**

A MOM'S FIGHT TO LIVE

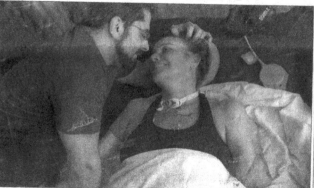

BILLY SMITH II i CHRONICLE

DEVOTION: There are times when Al and Katy Hayes share tears, but the fact that Katy is alive after suffering a massive, fast-moving infection that took all of her limbs is reason enough to smile.

After unimaginable tragedy followed the birth of her third child, she might not have seen this Mother's Day — but for one thing

T FIRST

CERS

The vow was till the end of time

By CINDY HORSWELL
HOUSTON CHRONICLE

A L Hayes recalled the day he stood in a century-old white chapel and made Katy his wife. It was a few months before the start of the new millennium, which some feared might signal the end of the world.

So, the Kingwood couple wrote wedding vows in which they promised to love each other and stay together "until the end of time."

Yet now, a decade later, Al finds himself seated before a computer to explain their commitment to each other in a blog.

His daily online musings began not long after he witnessed the home birth of their third child Feb. 10. But the joy of that moment

FAMILY PHOTO

MOMENT OF JOY: Katy Hayes had her daughter Arielle on Feb. 10. Only a few weeks later, Katy's arms and legs were amputated.

was quickly overshadowed when he found himself giving doctors permission to amputate his wife's legs and arms. To stop a raging infection spreading from

her uterus, doctors said her limbs had to be sacrificed or she would die.

He wrote later that signing the permission papers while Katy was in a coma was the hardest thing he ever did.

"I hope everyone will understand why I did this. I hope Katy will forgive me," he wrote.

To the dozen who wrote him that he should have just "let Katy go" or that "Katy wouldn't want to live like this," he responded: "You really don't know my wife."

Please see **MOTHER,** *Page A10*

WE LOVE MOM

This Mother's Day, Houstonians tell us about their favorite person — the one who sacrificed for her kids. **PAGE G1**

★**chron**.com **ONLINE:** Readers pay tribute to their moms. **momhouston.com**

"I'm realistic enough to know Katy will have down times and that she has some very tough rehab in her future. But I know how tenacious she is. She will rise to the challenge. She will prevail."

— AL HAYES

MOTHER: Goal is to go home, begin outpatient rehabilitation by June

BEFORE: Al and Katy Hayes — along with children Amber and Jake — were elated by the third pregnancy.

FAMILY PHOTO

CONTINUED FROM PAGE A1

Al and Katy Hayes were never conventional suburbanites.

Before marrying, Katy traveled the country in a Volkswagen van working on movie sets. One of her jobs was dressing the Teenage Mutant Ninja Turtles for the cameras. When she and her husband settled down in a two-story rental home in Kingwood to raise a family, she decided to hone her skills as a massage therapist and open a spa.

Her husband calls her his "granola girl," who adores nature, organic food, animals and, of course, children.

Al has a similar instinct for adventure. For 10 years, he's performed as a professional wrestler named Tony Vega, touring as one of the dynamic duo known as "Double Trouble."

He's also nurtured an interest in music that began when he taught himself to play the piano at age 6, later sharpening his skills at Columbia College in Chicago. When not slamming an opponent in the ring, he loves jam

SERENADE: Al Hayes, who teaches music at Pin Oak Middle School, goes over his own band's set list with his wife, Katy, on Wednesday at Parkland Hospital in Dallas. When Katy regained consciousness at the hospital, the last thing she remembered was giving birth.

BILLY SMITH II : CHRONICLE

barefoot in the grass again.

Later, he wrote in his blog that it hurts him every time he sees nail polish, shoes or rings. "I'm realistic enough to know Katy will have down times and that she has some very tough rehab in her future. But I know how tenacious she is. She will rise to the challenge. She will prevail."

Both have also been encouraged by the overwhelming support they've received at home. A friend has volunteered for the past several months to care for Arielle, while Al's sister, Betta Phelps, has helped with the other two. Dozens of fundraisers have covered the mounting bills.

"Perfect strangers have walked up and given us checks. It's amazing how giving people can be," said Katy's friend Silvey.

Purdue said Katy's was the worst case he's ever seen that didn't end in death.

"I think it's her attitude: What we have is what we make of it," the surgeon said.

■ ■ ■

play the piano at age 6, later sharpening his skills at Columbia College in Chicago. When not slamming an opponent in the ring, he loves jamming with his blues band. He also teaches music at Pin Oak Middle School in Bellaire.

The family's unorthodox life made a paradigm shift that surprised even them after Katy, at age 41, gave birth to their third child about three months ago.

Dawn Silvey, who met her at a Mothers of Young Children group, remembered Katy's exuberance over the pregnancy.

"She's such a happy, loving mother," Silvey said. "There is this light coming from her.. She just beams."

Katy's two other children — Amber, 16, and Jake, 6 — and Al were equally elated.

■ ■ ■

With the help of a midwife, Katy delivered the baby at home. She took no pain medication during the eight hours of labor before Arielle arrived, plump and healthy, tipping the scales at nearly 10 pounds.

Katy's muscles were sore, but the pain was no different from her previous births — until three days had passed.

"Then the pain changed to a more internal burning in the stomach, and her right shoulder started hurting real bad," Al said.

By the next morning, on Valentine's Day, the searing pain had grown more intense. Al took Katy to Kingwood Medical Center.

Lab results that came back the next day showed that Katy had invasive Group A Streptococcal disease — a rare, dangerously fast-spreading infection that sometimes preys on women weakened after a pregnancy. The milder version can lead to strep throat, but Katy had contracted two

SERENADE: Al Hayes, who teaches music at Pin Oak Middle School, goes over his own band's set list with his wife, Katy, on Wednesday at Parkland Hospital in Dallas. When Katy regained consciousness at the hospital, the last thing she remembered was giving birth.

BILLY SMITH II : CHRONICLE

FUNDRAISERS FOR THE HAYES FAMILY

■ **A Night at the Museum:** July 10 at the Houston Museum of Natural Science (music, auction, dinner)

■ **Donations:** Visit katyhayesfund.giving. officelive.com.

■ **Read Al Hayes' blog:** http://katyupdate. wordpress.com/

GLIMPSE OF HER DAUGHTERS: Katy leans back after looking at a photo of her two daughters, Amber, 16, and 3-month-old Arielle. Katy has seen her children only rarely since being hospitalized.

BILLY SMITH II : CHRONICLE

into a coma. She thrashed in her bed as her heart raced and her blood pressure remained dangerously low.

■ ■ ■

A doctor told Al several times that Katy had less than a 5 percent chance of living.

"I nicknamed him 'Dr. Five Percent' and told him that he didn't need to remind me again," Al recalled. "I was in disbelief. ... How could this happen?"

Later he learned the strep bacteria can be transmitted by coughing or sores on the skin. The midwife swabbed Katy's throat after the birth and a lab detected no strep, but doctors say it sometimes takes time to show up.

"It's just your day or not your day," said Dr. Gary Purdue, a surgeon at Parkland Hospital in Dallas. "You can scratch your head and get it. It's around us all the time."

Katy's condition continued to worsen. After 2½ gallons of infectious fluids were drained from her, doctors told Al that more drastic measures were needed to stop her insides from rotting.

On Katy's second day in

them."

■ ■ ■

On Feb. 24, Al arranged to airlift Katy to Parkland Hospital's burn trauma unit, which has more experience treating the flesh-eating bacteria.

She had been in Dallas only a couple of days when doctors asked Al to let them amputate Katy's limbs. He said no, firmly — at first.

He began seeking out other medical authorities, desperate for alternatives before time ran out for Katy.

The next day he learned one infection led to yet another, this one even more lethal: *purpura fulminans.* Doctors he contacted now concurred: The permanently damaged tissue on his wife's limbs had to be removed, or

ness March 12, the last thing she remembered was giving birth.

Agitated, she asked Al to get her out of there. That was when he told her about the surgeries. She took his words in silently, then said, "My baby doesn't know me yet."

"That's why we're fighting," Al reassured her.

Her first question was, "Are you OK?"

He could not believe she was worried about him.

Katy and Al have no regrets about having a home birth, because strep is often contracted in hospitals. They don't want to waste any energy looking back on what cannot be changed — although once in a while they have cried together, like when they realized she would never walk

barefoot in the grass again.

"I think it's her attitude: What we have is what we make of it," the surgeon said.

■ ■ ■

This past week, Katy improved so much that she was allowed to move from intensive care to the rehabilitation floor. Her goal is to grow strong enough to go home and start outpatient rehab by June.

In a regular room now, a smile lit Katy's face as she gazed up at her husband.

"He saved my life. I wouldn't be here without him," she whispered.

They kissed gently. Then he began his routine of massaging her shoulders and limbs with lavender oil. He scratched her nose when it itched and held her cup so she could sip through a straw.

"The hardest thing is not being able to do anything for yourself. I'm at the mercy of people," she said softly.

Another frustration has been not being able to hold Arielle when she visits. But now Katy is looking forward to a Mother's Day treat — seeing Amber and Jake, her old children, for just the second time.

Katy told her husband she wants foam pads put on the floor at home so she might slide around on them.

"As long as we're together we'll be OK," Al said.

Katy whispered back, "I'm so lucky, the family I have."

cindy.horswell@chron.com

Michelle,

Holy crap!
It's hard.

The End

(Happy Mother's Day to someone
who makes it look easy.)

Truly, you are an amazing
woman, mother, and friend.
It has been an honor
getting to know you.
Beth

Happy
Mother's Day
TO SOMEONE SPECIAL

All the kind and thoughtful
things you do can never
be honored enough.

Thank you for
all the love and care
you have given me.

Arielle

Michele,
Thank you for all that you are, and have, done for my family. I know that Arielle is getting _great_ care, and lots of _LOVING_! Happy Mother's Day!

Katy Hayes

great moms
grow great kids.
Thanks for helping to raise one of mine!

happy mother's day

A few days ago you started arching your back. I'll go to change your diaper and you'll just stiffen up and push your tummy to the sky. You seem quite pleased with yourself.

When you're ready to sleep, you roll to one side and suck your hand. This can be tricky if I'm changing your pants or your outfit.

There has been no adjustment time when it comes to your pack-n-play. Betta and Tom had the carpets cleaned and moved your nursery downstairs into your Mama's old massage office. Logistically, it will be better. Al talks of a rapid transition with you home full-time. Lots of mixed feelings and tender emotions.

Jennifer asked me to include her so she'd have an alibi.

Jennifer loving on Arielle

I missed you today. My life kept me so busy I didn't get to spend my usual day with you. Miss Zoe was thrilled to have you as her guest. Betta picked you up next. Betta returned and even put you to bed.

Miss Zoe was very complimentary about the care I was giving you. You have the sweetest nature. You are also getting enough sleep.

Tomorrow will be a big day for other reasons. Great surprises await!

Karen from church came over to tutor Sam in reading. We had invited her to stay for dinner. While I prepared dinner she fed you. Sam asked "What's Miss Karen doing?" and I replied "She's giving the bottle a baby".

Crazy, busy day. Your Dad stopped by for 35 minutes this morning. Gia took your three month pictures plus shots of you and me. Lunch with Sam. Lunch with Tom and Betta and Lucille. Family discussions about your transition, nursery and continued care. Bank. Groceries. 20 minute nap. Pick up kids. Snack. Homework. Play. Tutor. Dinner. Bath. Bed for you and Sam. Me? Dishes. Snacks. Paperwork. Phone calls. TV shows. Mail. Laundry.

Your Dad noticed how you like to cross your legs, flex your feet and pop your legs apart. And do it again and again and again.

Article in the paper touched me and I wrote them.

EDITORIAL / OPINIONS

Be that spark in someone else's life

Facebook, Twitter, reality TV shows, unlimited text messages, entertainment companies more focused on their bottom lines than their impact on young viewers, and so-called role models, with little regard to how their actions impact those who admire them.

Combine all that with the constantly changing face of the family structure in our community and more young people are "growing up" on their own or with little positive guidance.

Several months ago I mentioned that it "takes a village to raise a child." The phrase originated from an African proverb that I often heard growing up and it stuck with me.

The phrase was first introduced to some people when then-first lady of the United States Hillary Rodham Clinton titled her book "It Takes a Village: And Other Lessons Children Teach Us."

The following week after my column, I received a letter from an engaged reader who felt otherwise. He explained how it was actually my parents, grandparents and family that raised me to become the man I am today.

It was a sincere letter that led to a good dialogue, and I guess we agreed to disagree.

But I actually believe that phrase applies more today than it ever has before.

I certainly can't discredit the positive role my parents and family had on my life. Without them, I wouldn't be here and I wouldn't have the high expectation they created for my future.

But I also can't ignore the fact that so many other people in my life helped to raise me along the way. Everyone from the youth leaders at Mt. Zion Missionary Baptist Church to some of my youth sports coaches, to others in the community who felt they could play a positive role in my life.

I was always amazed growing up when we would take trips to visit my grandparents in Columbus and West Point, Miss. Like much of Mississippi, both of their cities were relatively small and it seemed everyone in the town at least knew who everyone else was.

But what amazed me growing up was how I eventually thought we were related to every single person in the city. I was only there once or twice a year and I couldn't even walk to the corner store or local park without several people recognizing that I was one of the Turners. Some seemed to know me so well they could tell the difference between me and my two younger brothers. Heck,

COREYTURNER

cturner@hcnonline.com

there are people in my family that struggle still with that one sometimes.

But hundreds of miles from "home" was a neighborhood of people who showed how much they care every time I visited. And although I was related to some, most had no connection to me.

I remember getting drilled by the old lady at the end of my grandma's block. "Are you hanging out with the right crowd out there in Texas?" "How is school coming along?" "Don't let me hear about you getting into some mess."

I didn't appreciate her yearly interrogations as a child, unless they were accompanied by her sweet potato pie. But I would love to have a conversation with her today.

I would ask why she was so interested in seeing me be successful. And it wasn't just me; she did the same for all of my cousins and I imagine others in the neighborhood. The funny thing is, she wasn't the only one to "keep us in line."

I got the same breakdown when we would visit our grandma's church or even at the grocery store. I would always ask if that was an aunt or uncle of ours, and it was typically someone who just knew the family from around the town.

Sure, these people didn't "raise" me, but they sure inspired me to be better. I often thought of not letting them down because they expected so much of me.

That is what I think we are missing today. With all our advanced technology, busy schedules and personal bubbles, many young people don't have the "village" I had growing up.

Thankfully there are organizations, mentors, others that make the time to give back. They should be commended, and those efforts must be supported.

But I miss the old lady that refused to let me take the wrong path in life.

It obviously isn't our responsibility to raise another person's child. But saying a few encouraging words and setting a standard for young people certainly doesn't hurt. In many cases, they may not get that anywhere else.

If we take pride in the young people in our community, we will be surprised how much more pride they take in our community. It will often be a reciprocated effort.

So say something positive or encouraging to a local student when you can.

3 months old

I recorded my shows this evening and watched them late. All of a sudden, your Mom and Dad are on TV. He's talking about saving her life and she's saying how grateful she is. Your parents have been on a journey few will ever be able to comprehend.

Gia dropped off two discs of images from yesterday's THREE MONTH photo shoot. I got goose bumps ~ they are simply lovely.

When we get a minute, I'd love to share some of my feelings about upcoming transitions. Getting you ready to live at your original home makes me excited and anxious and a bit confused. Lots of emotion.

The author of the newspaper article I responded to has asked to print my letter. It seems odd but I agreed to it.

IN YOUR OPINION

Meant for me?

Dear Editor:

I'm very proud of our village. Katy Hayes has been in the news a lot lately. She is the new mom who contracted a deadly form of Strep A in her bloodstream, had multiple organ failure and has had all four limbs amputated. I have her baby.

Arielle has been under my care for more than three months and I have not been alone for one step.

Kingwood, its people, businesses, churches and strangers have supported the Hayes family and my efforts with baby Arielle. We have been gifted with hours of loving support. People come to hold the baby, help with housework, gardening, bring casseroles, gift cards and baby supplies. All of this baby's needs have been met by this community.

It does take a village to raise a child. We have such a village. The compassion that people have shown touches me greatly. With this outpouring of love and support, I can attest to the cherished disposition inherent in a baby who instead of being with her mother is with her "other."

I can't claim to be a spark in anybody's life. I am the hands that do the work and the smile in the wee hours of Arielle's life. Out of tragedy, I have had an amazing opportunity to mother a baby who needed mothering.

As a single mother, I hope that I am teaching my young son a valuable lesson in compassion. Raising another's child might not be the popular choice in society, but a calling and a need so compelling has to scoff at tradition.

Not our responsibility to raise another's child? And yet we are doing it. From me, this community family will have my eternal grati-

tude and respect.

Michele Dykstra
Kingwood

Great day for charity

Dear Editor:

The Tuesday after Mother's Day, a clear day with a slight breeze, found 100 women who came together to play for charity at Kingwood Country Club's Tennis Center in the second annual Society of St. Stephen Tennis Tournament.

With the opportunity to win the grand prize, affording the winner a day at the Kingwood Country Club Day Spa for four (donated by the Clubs of Kingwood), nearly 100 door prizes and amazing raffle baskets and spectacular silent auction items donated by Kingwood, Humble and Atascocita area businesses, HTLA teams and individuals alike, the players headed out to the courts for a day of fun in the sun.

Overseeing all of the tennis pairings and working closely for months with the tournament committee, staff and management of Kingwood Country Club, club tennis pro Randy Mattingley assisted the committee in every aspect of the tournament in order to make the day a great success.

Organized expertly by tournament coordinators Jim and Diana Rutherford, the Society of St. Stephen Tennis Tournament Committee and the staff at Kingwood Country Club and the Tennis Center, the event went off beautifully and raised over $30,000 for the ongoing financial needs of the all-volunteer, 501(c)(3) Society of St. Stephen, most notably the school supplies drive coming up in August.

The school supplies drive will give more than 500 children in the area their school sup-

See **LETTERS**, Page 6A

A gorgeous, breezy day capped off by a rainy, stormy night.

Another busy day and another TV interview. Tiffany at Channel 11 did a great job. Talked to your Mom today. It's great getting to visit with her.

You and Sam have been starting your days extra early. This morning he got you out of your pack-n-play, strapped you into your pillow/recliner and was sitting next to you playing a video game. I was upset he picked you up but overwhelmed with the love and care he shows you. He'll be a fine Dad one day.

Sam comforts Arielle

Ah! Here I sit at 10:30 p.m. writing to you Baby Arielle, and to you Katy. You've spent the afternoon and this night, at your family's house. Aunt Betta has lovingly fashioned an amazing nursery for your homecoming. Even with you gone, our actions still include you. Plenty of pukey laundry, restocking supplies, computer work and phone calls. Thank you for the break. I miss you :) but it's given me one-on-one time with Sam.

Al (your Dad) says they will be home Tuesday. It's so exciting. Everyone is working so hard to get things ready for your Mom's return.

Larry (Mary Kay's Dad) calls with dreams of buying some land and building a home for Baby Arielle and Katy to live in with their family. He mows your lawn now but is passionate about this new endeavor.

Job opportunity (hotel sales) popped up for me. What do I do?

It is my great fortune that Sam is seven years old and therefore I am required to check on him seven times each night (I say with a wink). His small nightlight gives off just enough glow so I can see his features softened by sleep. Listening to him breath, I fix his covers and smile with a contentment I cannot fully express. I love being Sam's Mom.

In his room, my mind wanders to the possibility of a job for me. A grown-up job, outside the home providing resources to help cover the expenses of life and the lawsuit. A girlfriend called to say she had recommended me for a fantastic opportunity and encouraged me to pursue it. She told me I had to think of my own future and just give the baby back. How simple that sounds. With Katy improving by leaps and bounds, I am optimistic that Arielle really will have a life with her family someday. How would that unfold? Do you really just return a baby like a blouse that doesn't match? How would this affect my son? After careful consideration, I decide a baby step is in order and submit my application. But emotionally, I was on the fence. That particular job was not meant for me after all. Relief and reassurance that I was doing exactly what I was supposed to be doing with my life brought me some peace. When the time is right, I know I will find the right work situation that balances my priorities.

There are times when I question if taking the baby was the right thing to do as far as Sam is concerned. Personally, I think it has been an amazing experience for him and he truly loves her. Sam's capacity for genuine kindness and thoughtfulness never ceases to make my chest swell with pride. Whether the situation is ideal isn't really the point. The lawsuit that threatens his home, his comfort zone, his security and his relationship with his mother seem far more treacherous than a tiny, new, pink baby.

None of these thoughts disturb his sleep as he rolls over and splays his long frame diagonally across his twin bed, a foot sticking out from under the covers. Heading back downstairs with a smile on my face I go back to my evening chores. I get six more check-in visits before I go to bed and I couldn't be happier about it.

Last night, while you slept at your home, I dreamt about your Mom. I dreamt about her at her house with you in the nursery. I dreamed she held you in her arms. Every dream, she was in a wheelchair, but she was smiling and holding you. I dreamed you all came to church with me and I interrupted service taking a picture of you and your Mom. It's all good.

I missed you last night. Betta retuned you all dressed for bed in my favorite sack and I got all choked up. I know our time is coming to an end soon ~ or at least a colossal revolution. Hopefully, you leave feeling CHERISHED.

A wonderful day indeed and several poignant pukings. It is so fun to dress-up little baby girls. We get to put on ruffled bottoms, bold patterns and sassy bows. Too cute!

The big news (that <u>many</u> people know) and we're "supposed" to keep quiet, is that your Mama is suppose to come home tomorrow. With luck, she'll be home late afternoon. Originally, your Dad asked me to just drop you off and thanks. After reconsidering the many challenges your family will be facing, he asked me to continue with the afternoon visitation schedule but full weekend visits with them. I have agreed to and support this arrangement for you. I'm so not ready to say good-bye.

Trimmed your fingernails today and you didn't scream at all.

What will I say when I get to see your Mama? "Katy, you made the most wonderful, beautiful, happiest, delightful baby ever. But she pukes a lot".

HUGE developments. <u>Katy came home</u>. You were there waiting for her too. I put you in your cutest outfit and got you all ready to go. What a reunion that must have been! :)

PEOPLE magazine called tonight. They want the world to know about your amazing Mom and her courageous spirit.

It's been an overwhelming day. I'm thrilled and exhausted. Let's sleep well tonight, tomorrow is a brand new day.

Sam's silver dollar.

The big snafu today was that I thought you might be sick. You aren't. You've just had a couple tough nights and were not your usual self. Even had Noel come check you out. I'm so glad you're well.

I have turtle pee on my feet. It's not how I normally end the day but it's not everyday I rescue a turtle as big as my head out of the middle of the road. I guess the relocation was stressful on Mr. Turtle. Who knew a turtle could hold that much pee?

Your Dad brought you home tonight and we had a great chat. Lots of communication to help all of us.

Al and his baby girl

You slept through the night ~ like an angel. We went through your morning routine but today, they picked you up at 9:30 a.m. It feels so strange to run errands without you. Your Mom had a rough morning. When Betta left to come get you, your Mom was hurting, nauseous and crying. I can't imagine the hurts on the outside, much less, the hurts on the inside. Back again tonight and I'm feeling a little mixed up. I'm not sure what my role is any more. I'm just trying to be supportive and do what's best. Started packing up a bit of your excess. Been focusing on "good" for you (back with your family) and "good" for me (getting my life back). It's still a lot to take in sweetie. Going to visit your Mama tomorrow morning. Can't wait any longer to see her.

Thank you for sleeping through the night last night. We had our morning routine, including our weekly visit from Tracy. I took you over to the house this morning and got to see your Mom. I presented you to her and we laughed, we cried, we hugged, we kissed and we shared a moment. It felt good. I tried making your Mom laugh and we just had a good gab for around an hour and 20 minutes. Kayla was there and she helped me unload some baby stuff.

The transitioning is taking a different direction than was anticipated. Lots of worries over you my dear. Who will care for you once you "go home"? Betta walked me to the car and spoke honestly about your Mom's struggles and pain. Tonight, she and Tom stayed for an hour visiting about what the near future hold for the Hayes.

Britt brought a bottle of wine and we just talked. The good, the bad and the ugly.

Need to shower, feed you and pass out. It's almost midnight. Today held more than I can write. Let's see how tomorrow unfolds.

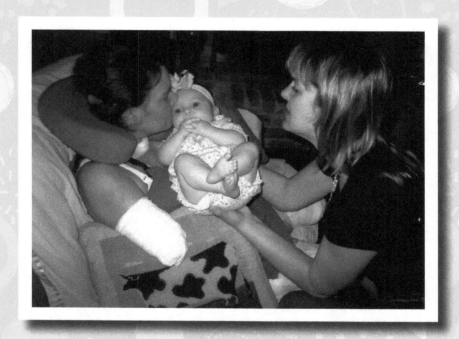

Katy, Arielle and Michele

This is the morning. Our last morning. Your trial weekend away. Your Daddy is coming at 9:30 a.m.

I have become obsolete. Seemingly replaced by a mother with no arms and no legs and requiring round the clock care. Are they ready? Arielle came into my life so completely and for three entire months, or was it only three measly months? When our time seemed eternal I found a way to manage it all and with the end approaching I just feel uncertainty. Too many questions and unaddressed emotions cloud my mind to truly embrace the inevitable.

That Friday morning started as any other. But as the dogs start barking, I know he is close. With Clive and Nixon secured in the bedroom, I wait for him to ring the doorbell. Perhaps it was a formality or perhaps I am just truly stalling. Maybe I am trying to convince myself "she's mine" for the next twenty seconds until I open the door. She's grown so much she's heavy in my arms. Or maybe she's light in my arms because I'm getting used to the weight. Maybe all these contradictions are another stalling mechanism because I haven't fully accepted the demise of my role or the next unimaginable step. They say having a baby means you wear your heart outside your body. Now I am tasked with the parting of my borrowed child, a piece of my heart, my baby girl Arielle.

He gathers his child with a smile seemingly oblivious to all the efforts made to ready her and the internal war of emotions that rage inside my socially correct demeanor. My smile is genuine with happiness for my friends and their child, but also a careful mask to hide my heart's true feelings.

I watch him walk down the front path, away from me, with my baby. My sweet baby girl. The baby carrier swings from his right hand. The yellow baby blanket hangs over his left shoulder, her head over his shoulder and she stares at me as he walks down the front path toward his car. She is very alert, sucking her fingers and taking in her surroundings. It had been a typical morning for us with a baby bath, a little lotion massage and a clean outfit. I had fed her and burped her but she still wound up soaking her outfit. With care I chose a special outfit and had dressed her in a pale green and light blue cotton set. Maybe not the most feminine for a three-month old girl but it had such cute details and ruffles on the bottom. He's taking my baby. Turning over his shoulder he smiles and says good-bye. My baby. It was a beautiful, sunny, Texas morning. A beautiful morning, except today, he had come to take my baby.

She hadn't always been my baby. She wasn't my baby when I picked her up at her house. She wasn't my baby when I visited her mother in the ICU. She wasn't my baby for many sleepless nights. But during this unconventional and unexpected journey, she became my baby. There were so many times I thought her Mom might not make it. How could she die and leave a newborn behind? Maybe that is when I decided to take Arielle not only into my home and my life, but into my heart. She would be mine and in return, I would be hers.

He has taken my baby. He buckles her into the car seat and I wonder if the neighbors can see my anguish. But there are no witnesses to our separation. Tucked safely in their homes, they are immune to my grief. He is taking my baby to his house. To be with him, her father and Katy, her real mother. The people who planned her, named her, sang to her before she was born, loved her before she seemed real. She has a brother and a sister anxious to start their life with her as part of the family. But this baby, this sweet, babbling, baby girl is leaving me. He is taking her away from me. I smile as my heart breaks. My mind understands the logistics, but my heart is screaming. Could I stop him? No, she is not truly mine to claim. Yet, I know, and secretly hoped that this day would come. The empty pit in my stomach is additional confirmation of my predicament and heartache. Again, I scan the street for witnesses but for all outward appearances, all is well. I take a deep breath and go back inside my house. After all, I am not her mother, I have only been her "other".

Epilogue

Morning turned into night and the day came to a close. It wasn't that day or the next that I stopped reaching for her or listening for her sounds in the middle of the night. Days turn into weeks and evidence of her still dots our home and every conversation. But slowly, very slowly, my heart learned to let go a little more each day. And while the entirety of her three-month visit was incomprehensible, she has filled me with pink love. Who knew an extended stay from this little baby girl would change the course of my life and teach me new affection? I was humbled by this experience, grateful to the family that chose me and linked by this experience to my little pink houseguest.

And while I can never tell "Katy's Story" for truly that is hers to tell, I can't talk about baby Arielle without feeling immense and profound appreciation for the many people who lovingly helped us along. From friends to strangers, church groups to neighbors and the dozens of people I didn't even mention, I am forever grateful to the Kingwood community.

I have found in life that often you think your purpose or your path is a specific thing only to find it was something else entirely. Was Arielle a gift so I could be a girl mom? Or was her stay part of Al and Katy's story? Or was it to show the depth and immeasurable goodness of people? Of community at its finest? Regardless, I now get to thank you for letting me share my story. Because every time I share this "very unexpected journey" I get to relive helping my dear friends, I get to feel myself falling in love with Arielle and I get to remember when things went right and a little pink baby was reunited with her family.

THE END